AF391678

INSPIRING STORIES OF
GROWTH AND SYNCHRONICITY

DARING
metamorphosis

AN ANTHOLOGY OF 20 VOICES

COMPILED BY

SOPHIE ROUMÉAS

Daring Metamorphosis
An anthology of twenty voices
Sophie Rouméas

Published by Angel Lab Editions
Angel Lab Editions is a brand and division of SBR Coaching & Resources, Annecy, France
www.angellabeditions.com

Translated from English to French by Marine Armstrong
Translated from French to English by Crystal Weber
Edited and revised by Claude Jameux
Final French proofreading by Marine Armstrong and Renée Rembarz
Final English proofreading by Crystal Weber
Original cover design by Darko Dojchinovski

SEL031000   SELF-HELP / Personal Growth / General
SEL023000   SELF-HELP / Personal Growth / Self-Esteem
HEA055000   HEALTH & FITNESS / Mental Health

English Edition:
ISBN: 978-2-9578712-4-7 (paperback) | 978-2-9578712-7-8 (ebook)

French Edition:
ISBN: 978-2-9578712-5-4 (paperback) | 978-2-9578712-6-1 (ebook)

DEDICATION

Metamorphosis is loving oneself fully,
in the silence of the mirror,
It is accepting, transforming, and revealing oneself,
independent of another's gaze.
It is loving the other without expecting them
to rely on our reflection,
And gently helping them find their own light.
It is moving forward together, free from the game of mirrors,
And appreciating the other beyond the mirror,
Whatever their facets may be.

To you who read us, to us who write to you,
To those who have been, those who are, and those who will be,
With gratitude, resonance, and transformation—let us dare.

INTRODUCTION

THE IDEA BEHIND THE BOOK AND ITS ORIGINS

The idea for *Daring Metamorphosis* took root amidst the global pandemic that affected us starting in 2020. That period of confinement, which imposed an intimate proximity with oneself, awakened existential questions for many: *Do I love my life? Am I happy in my work? Does my daily routine hold meaning?*

For others, it was an opportunity for introspection, action, and transformation: working from home, building online networks, incorporating hobbies and passions long forgotten into daily life, or even choosing a new place to live to navigate this unprecedented time. Some decided to change careers; others turned constraints into opportunities. This kaleidoscope of changes fascinated me.

By 2021, fragments of this book, a collective work from its very inception, began to take shape on my computer. Yet it wasn't until early 2024 that the evidence became clear: *the time is now.* Synchronicities multiplied, and meaningful encounters— friends, colleagues, and even a young woman I met by chance in an art gallery — confirmed this impulse.

This book exists thanks to collective effort, bringing together stories where change, sometimes unexpected, reveals the profound depth of human potential.

THE COMMON THREAD OF METAMORPHOSIS

At the heart of the chapters in this anthology lies a common thread: the need to refocus on oneself and to listen to one's inner voice. The timeless maxim *"know thyself"* is one of the essential foundations of metamorphosis. Many paths lead to this journey, each unique and personal, yet all deeply rooted in self-awareness and introspection.

Dreams: A gateway to transformation

Dreams are one of these paths. A multidimensional realm of the psyche, they act both independently of and in connection with our conscious thoughts. Each night, our awareness shifts from ordinary perception to the dream world, transforming our waking self into a dreamer. Dreams weave scenarios that often symbolically reflect our psychological and emotional processes.

The psyche is defined as the entirety of conscious and unconscious processes unique to each individual. However, the dictionary also refers to the psyche as a mirror— a pivoting object that reflects our image from different angles— or as a butterfly, a symbol of transformation. These three definitions converge toward the changing and multidimensional nature of the human soul.

Thus, the transition between wakefulness and dreams contains the very essence of metamorphosis. It is a passage, an invitation to keep our awareness alive throughout the process, to observe how the dream world, freed from the constraints of matter, becomes a space of pure transformation. This daily loop, from Alpha to Omega, reminds us that each day is an opportunity for renewal—whether we remember our dreams or not.

Daytime observation

Metamorphosis is not confined to the world of dreams. For many, it finds fertile ground in self-observation during the day, particularly through our internal dialogues. These exchanges, often influenced by unconscious memories, are colored by the "little voices" inherited from childhood: "be strong," "try harder," "be perfect," "hurry up," "please others." These injunctions, whether silent or spoken, reflect the expectations of authority figures who shaped our development.

To protect itself, the inner child adopts masks— defense mechanisms that persist into adulthood. While these masks may have been essential for surviving past traumas, they often become unconscious barriers to the expression of our authenticity. They blend with our personality without being innate. Instead, they limit our freedom to be ourselves and trap us in relational patterns where we grant others the power to define us.

In *The Five Wounds That Prevent You from Being Yourself*, Lise Bourbeau, describes these masks as follows:

1. **Betrayal:** Fear of separation,

   represented by the mask of control.

2. **Rejection:** Fear of panic at being rejected, represented by the mask of avoidance.

3. **Abandonment:** Fear of loneliness, represented by the mask of dependence.

4. **Humiliation:** Fear of freedom, represented by the mask of masochism.

5. **Injustice:** Fear of coldness, represented by the mask of rigidity.

To rediscover our authenticity, it is necessary to remove these masks and heal the underlying wounds. This requires conscious effort, choosing to act not from these defense mechanisms but in alignment with our deepest aspirations. Carl Jung referred to this as the path of individuation, *"moving away from masks and closer to the heart."*

FAMILY MAPS AND INVISIBLE LOYALTIES: THE IMPACT OF FAMILIAL AND SOCIETAL SYSTEMS

Our lives are deeply influenced by family maps— intimate geographies silently passed down from generation to generation. These maps contain the values, beliefs, and responses to events from the familial past. They form what I call *silent education,* an invisible heritage that shapes our choices, often unconsciously.

While these invisible loyalties initially provide protection and a sense of belonging, they can also become chains. Out of love for our clan, we sometimes remain trapped in repetitive patterns that limit our freedom to be ourselves. Nevertheless, someone in an abusive relationship may, with the right support, dare to break free and update their internal programming. This process requires reconfiguring neural pathways, much like choosing new roads after years of traveling familiar ones. Changing paths means daring to select a more nourishing landscape and a direction more aligned with our soul.

These familial dynamics are not limited to the individual. They resonate on the scale of communities, societies, and even nations. Every social system carries indeed a collective heritage of values and beliefs, but also of wounds, conflicts, and injustices. These silent transmissions profoundly shape our lives, creating patterns that can confine as much as they protect.

The history of the world vividly illustrates these intergenerational and collective resonances. However, on an individual level, each act of consciousness and personal transformation helps to lighten these invisible chains. By revisiting our family maps, they can become valuable tools for illuminating our paths and fostering a more harmonious evolution for future generations.

TRAUMA AND HEALING: A HOLISTIC JOURNEY

Healing is not limited to tools or techniques; it requires deep understanding, a safe space to be seen, heard, and accepted in one's authenticity— whether broken or whole, luminous or shadowed.

Healing is a holistic process, like a hologram— but in five-dimensions, encompassing:

1. **The body,** a memory map where wounds and pains, even silent ones, are imprinted.

2. **The mind,** which sometimes needs to dismantle automatic neural patterns.

3. **The soul,** in search of meaning and connection beyond trauma.

4. **The external context,** both familial and societal, influencing every step.

5. **The universe,** where synchronicities play a key role.

METAMORPHOSIS: A PATH TO AUTHENTICITY

Metamorphosis is daring to break free from the psychological envelope imposed by external expectations. It is becoming free to evolve in alignment with one's conscience and values. This requires recognizing the influences of the various systems that shape our lives: family, community, religion, nation… and liberating ourselves from the ties that no longer resonate with us.

As we discover our inner truth, we harmonize our place in the world. This unique signature of the soul becomes its own melody, creating a fulfilling life aligned with our values and true aspirations.

The universe, much like the butterfly, is in perpetual transformation. It teaches us that every step, even the difficult ones, is part of a greater cycle where expansion and light reveal themselves at the right moment. By embracing these cycles, we become capable of leaving behind what no longer serves us, spreading our wings, and discovering the freedom and the love of our true essence.

METAMORPHOSIS: A UNIVERSAL AND MULTIDIMENSIONAL PROCESS

Metamorphoses are present in every human life. They may be triggered by a significant event, a crisis, or emerge more subtly within the folds of the psyche and dreams. They symbolize the deep and continuous journey of *becoming*, where every step, no matter how challenging, is essential to growth. Thus, metamorphosis represents the courage to leave the familiar and welcome new understandings of self, meaning, and connection to the world.

Meta, Morphè, Osis: The dimensions of metamorphosis

The word *metamorphosis* carries within it the fundamental steps of all transformation, inviting us to action.

Meta – Why?

Metamorphosis begins with deep reflection on the meaning of our experiences. This stage invites a quest for consciousness, an exploration of the motivations that inspire change. It is the transcendence of immediate perception to envision a broader view of oneself and the world.

Morphê – How?

From the form *morphê, eidos, logos* in Greek to Morphée (the God of dreams in Greek mythology), the passage occurs naturally, reflecting how we evolve through our moments of awareness. These philosophical concepts, rooted in ideas of structure and essence, underscore that every transformation is a meeting between our inner form and the external world.

This transformation, guided by a "meta" perspective, expands our understanding of ourselves and the world. It manifests in a sincere engagement with the process of change: navigating resistance, challenges, and learning to allow the evolution that calls to us. Form, whether visible or subtle, becomes the site of constant dialogue, a dance of adaptation and growth reflecting harmony between the internal and external.

Osis – What?

Metamorphosis is not merely a state of change; it is a process that demands action, courage, and intention. Rooted in the Greek *osis*, meaning "doing" or "process," this dimension of transformation invites us to take bold steps, leave the familiar behind, and confront the unknown.

It is through daring to act— however small or monumental the step— that potential becomes reality. In embracing this active journey, we uncover our inner light and, in doing so, contribute to illuminating the paths around us and with others.

Osis reminds us that transformation is not passive, it is a movement, a choice, and an ongoing commitment to growth and discovery.

Thus, from introspection to action, from dreaming to awakening, metamorphosis is a continuous and multidimensional process. It invites us to grow, push the limits of our psyche, and embrace our true essence with confidence and clarity.

Metamorphosis and book structure: A revealing synchronicity

The three stages of metamorphosis form the foundation for the organization of this book: through a beautiful synchronicity, the structure of the book itself mirrors the graphic symbol of metamorphosis— "the butterfly":

> Part One – The Why – comprising six chapters
> Part Two – The How – comprising seven chapters
> Part Three – The What – comprising six chapters

The unity of the book's organizational principle honors the diversity of its contributions: You will discover stories from twenty authors living in Austria, Bhutan, France - including an author in Tahiti, Canada, Portugal, Switzerland and the United States. While each testimony explores the three stages of metamorphosis, a primary focus emerges in each one, allowing for its seamless and natural integration into one of the book's sections.

AN INVITATION TO INNER LIGHT AND ACTION

These authentic and heartfelt stories offer a message of hope and solidarity to all those journeying through their own metamorphosis. They illustrate the power of personal transformation, emotional healing, and the ability to cultivate deeper, more aligned relationships.

By exploring these narratives, each reader can find inspiration to discover their own radiant resilience— an inner light that guides us through challenges and connects us to others. Each person who finds their path, driven by a life mission aligned with their heart, becomes in turn a source of hope and encouragement for and with those around them.

This book is both an illustration and a celebration of the human capacity to evolve, transform, and illuminate our surroundings, even through small actions. It is filled with profound gratitude for these shared stories and for the light that each of us carries within, often without even realizing it.

May these stories inspire you, resonate with your own journey— whether already clear or still unfolding— and help you discover the next words to write a new chapter of your story.

Sophie Rouméas

TABLE OF CONTENTS

PART TWO: MORPHE – HOW?

PART THREE: OSIS – WHAT?

Isabelle Estournet-Djehizian

SPREADING YOUR WINGS WIDE

I was born in 1962 in Marseille to an Armenian mother and a father from the Pyrenees. Since childhood, I have loved books, music, and drawing.

I want to tell you that it is never too late to be free.

For many years, I was a businesswoman, but after the deaths of my older brother—almost my twin—and then my mother, I fell apart.

Coming back from the abyss, an instinct awakened in me: the one that tells you that there is no more time to waste, that you can no longer pretend, that your life rings hollow. I became aware of my own prisons, moved forward, stumbled, and sought meaning. I began to uncover my hidden Armenian origins, my history. I dared to express what I felt, and little by little, I found my voice through words: I wrote my first book as if diving headfirst into life.

Thanks to my partner, my loyal readers, and the wonderful encounters that now mark my journey, I have chosen to do only one thing: to write and share the powerful tool that is the Word.

Today, after publishing a trilogy—*Momig, la Petite Bougie* (2014), *Le Ventre et la Plume* (2015), and *Que ma Voix Demeure* (2017), which gave rise to a play—I have just completed my first novel, *Dans les Harpes du Vent*.

My greatest joy? It's when someone tells me that my writing touched them and helped them find the strength to set out on their own journey.

You can also find me:
on my blog: www.auvifdemaplume.fr
on the Momig Facebook page:
https://www.facebook.com/momig.lapetitebougie
and discover my books: www.lagriffedevinaya.fr

Isabelle Estournet-Djehizian

SPREADING YOUR WINGS WIDE

Descendant of Eastern Christians

Granddaughter of Armenian orphans

Daughter of mathematicians

I once believed myself an accountant

When in truth, I am a storyteller

And this realization brings me joy

For I wish to remember

That the man who, one day, entered my grandfather's home

With a sword in hand

Also has, somewhere on this planet,

A granddaughter to whom he has said nothing.

—Isabelle Estournet-Djehizian

AUGUST 26, 2024

First times are always difficult: a first cry, a first glance, a first step, a first fall. Today, I honor our first meeting in the heart of this collective project with both joy and apprehension.

I have already crossed the dark forest of words to find my path: my first book *Momig, La Petite Bougie* was born under my pen in 2014. Beyond the joy of its mere existence, it gently gave me a name that suits me well, a name under which I now sign.

The 'birth' was as difficult as that of my first child, but then nothing could stop me, and it was quickly followed by its little siblings *Le Ventre et la Plume* and *Que ma Voix Demeure*. And when I look at what I have received from the hundreds of readers who dared to welcome this unique writing style with open eyes and hearts, I know that this path is truly mine and that I simply need the courage to continue.

I speak of courage because life requires so much to find one's freedom: the courage to take responsibility, the courage to speak with respect, the courage to listen with kindness. It's so much easier to stay silent and endure, or to endure and complain—that's what I did for a long time. And then one day, you no longer like what you have become, you look at yourself and don't recognize yourself: 'Is this me, this embittered woman? This exhausted entrepreneur? This breathless mother? This wife who no longer knows how to love?'

I remember when the children were young, and we walked through crowded streets, we would say to them, 'If you get lost, don't be afraid. Go back to the last place you saw us. We'll be waiting for you there.'

It's that place where, one day, you must return—the place where you took a path that wasn't yours. You must do it without fear, with humility and kindness toward yourself.

This journey marked by reading and writing is the one I offer to share with you today. Perhaps you'll want to share yours with me, with us? It's so much easier when we feel less alone.

APRIL 8, 2013

My mother was born in Marseille to parents who, as children, survived the Armenian genocide.

Her father crossed Der Zor, the terrible desert where men driven by hatred made men crazed with grief perish. Bought for a few pennies by a Red or Blue Cross, my grandfather journeyed through life as an orphan.

Her mother remained silent all her life, keeping everything deep in her throat, deep in her heart; she neither whispered nor sang. She simply passed down, through her daughter's breath, her fears, her sorrows, her exile.

My mother inherited it all: In the silence of her parents' labor-filled days, dedicated to making her a princess, she heard the violence, the mourning, the abandonment, the exile. But hidden beneath these, she also sensed the lands, the winds, and the dust of unknown Armenia—this forbidden word. 'My little French girl,' her father would say, looking at her with pride. So, she held this silence they had given her in the hollow of her heart and kept all her questions to herself.

I was born of this breath, for we are always born from our mother's breath. With a cry, she brought me into the world, and my cry answered hers: Yes, I will be alive, and I will bear, like you, the burden of silence. I will say nothing, and all will be well, yes, all will be well.

I was born of this silence—a silence so loud that it prevented me, too, from hearing the murmur of life, of my desires. But memory resists everything: the silence of elders, the tides of history, the betrayals of the powerful, the changes of territory, the fading of language, the weariness of poetry.

And when the impossible finally happened, when at last Mother spoke, it was nothing but a cry: 'Help me!' she screamed, then wrote it on the walls of her hospital room before she passed away.

That day, I knew that the only way to tame this beast we unknowingly carry within in is to tear the veil and drag this hundred-headed monster out of the void.

To break the silence, with small, very small steps, I came into writing.

MAY 12, 2013

I land in Armenia, in every sense of the word. No member of my family has ever set foot in this part of the world before me.

My suitcase is heavy.

One has to be in the middle of their life to dare to confront all of this.

Fields stretch out as far as the eye can see, faithfully following the rises and falls of the Vayots Dzor valley. This land vibrates, without a doubt—I can feel it.

I approach a small bush—which one of us chooses the other? Its roots gently anchor into the earth in a delicate network of filaments. Its many branches, burned by winter, already carry their promise of the future. They hold each other, all stemming from the same base. The light breath of the wind passing through the bush fills me with a strange music:

Like me, you root yourself in the earth

All of humanity lies beneath your feet, do you feel it?

Your branches are budding, your flowers will soon bloom

It's time to look beneath

To discover your roots

To honor your ancestors, yes

To meet them, to uncover the humus...

Time has laid thousands of stories beneath you

Magnificent flowers that have faded

Ashes of joyful fires

Bruised leaves, severed branches

Heaps of fragrant plants

And all has decayed

Time is the ultimate master; we need only wait...

Summers and winters pass

The ground settles

Colors fade, all takes on the same shade

And all sinks further

Penetrating the earth without leaving a trace

But one day, delicately,

A new substance emerges

Rich from all these pasts brought together

Flocculent, alive, vibrant

It's light, soft, and warm all at once

Fragrant like a spring morning

Like a newborn child who always smiles at life

It is humus, humanity, a tree, human, you, me.

I hold a sprig of the blooming bush in my hand. I am ready to continue my journey.

MAY 15, 2013

I lit candles in every monastery

And I cried

I let the tears flow

I let the tears dry

I watched the candles burn

Thinking of each of you, my departed

You, my brother; you, my mother

And your parents who left this place

And your grandparents who died here, somewhere, in a desert

I found comfort in seeing these small flames come

Blacken the thick walls of these mountain refuges,
*   perched up high*

Beacons in my night, waiting so patiently for me

When will she finally take the road that leads to us?

I lit candles in every monastery

And I smiled

I let the dead rest in peace

I let memories gently drift into slumber

I watched the candles burn

Thinking of each of you, my living ones,

My ships that now travel and carry in the depths of their eyes

This little piece of land, this little flame whose story I shared
*   with you.*

I lit candles in every monastery
From Khor Virap to Tatev
And I soared high into the sky
Grateful to have found my wings again.

JUNE 21, 2013

This morning, I invited light to enter me.

It may seem strange, but the intention I put into this prayer made the light truly enter. It seeped into every part of my body, softly illuminating each pulse of the extraordinary alchemy that makes me a living being.

I welcomed it and let it flow from head to toe, gently exploring my inner self, from which I often drift away—as if I had a choice. Like a host receiving a guest, I put on a good face: I opened closed doors for it and let it reach the dark corners; I accompanied it in its free dance and greeted the mysterious places along the way. It felt as if I were treading unknown land, and truth be told, the journey was long for someone as impatient as I am. But who could boast of traveling at the speed of light?

This morning, I invited light to enter me.

It didn't take me long to realize that this subtle shift of my presence in the world—from the outside to the inside—provoked a feeling close to panic in me. I was tempted to open my eyes to anchor myself back in the present. What is more reassuring than the object you see immediately in front of you? But an instinctive trust in the process, mingled with a childlike curiosity, convinced me to persevere. As I made space for it, I felt the light expanding my inner space, as though, among its many talents, it could also push back walls.

This morning, I invited light to enter me.

It didn't come alone. It was accompanied by Patience and Kindness, its two lifelong friends. For a long time, my door was invisible to them. For a long time, I didn't have the energy to welcome them, too busy gasping, chasing after the ticking of the clock. 'I'm overwhelmed... I'm drowning...'

But this morning, all three were there, and I admit I felt a strong desire to renew the experience the very next day.

This morning, I invited light to enter me. I just wanted to share this experience with you; the light is so generous.

AUGUST 15, 2013

Dinner lingers on under the stars, the evening is mild. It's been a tough day: thirteen kilometers in the mountains, climbing, twisting, descending. Jean-Pierre, my companion, looks fresh. With his long legs, he swallows up kilometers far smaller than ours. Our guest, the painter Hovhannes, is half-dead with exhaustion.

The flames of the little candles on the table are the only movements in the night. Silence has settled, each of us content thinking about our own mountain.

- "Who are you?" Hovhannes turns to me and softly asks the question in his deep voice. "Yes, who are you?"

Jean-Pierre looks at me, amused. At last, we've reached the heart of the matter—'Who are you?' holds so many questions.

Daughter of…, mother of…, partner of…, a girl who sings…, who loves the mountains… it all swirls in my mind, but I say nothing. No, this 'Who are you?' does not call for those answers, I feel it.

Chin resting on my hands, I wait. I wait to find the answer that Hovhannes deserves. Jean-Pierre says nothing either; the moment is solemn, and he won't come to my rescue.

Then I point to a candle dripping its wax onto the table:

- "That's what I am."
- "A candle?" Hovhannes asks.
- "Yes, that's it. I am this little candle, spreading its light and warmth, that's all."
- "Alright," Hovhannes says to me, "and what do you do with it?"
- "I write. I keep a journal. Well, I write for myself, what I see, what I feel. In fact, I wrote something about you the day I posed for you, I wrote."
- "Would you read it to me, please, Isabeldjan?"

Taking my journal, I begin:

July 18, 2013: I posed nude for Hovhannes...

When I finish reading what I had written that day, Hovhannes looks at me and says,

- "It's incredible, that's exactly it. Everything is there, you captured it all in just a few words. It's certain, Isabeldjan, you are a writer."

OCTOBER 15, 2013

La Griffe de Vinaya is born, "Griffe" as a signature, a decisive mark on destiny.

I entrusted my texts to Vincent to work on graphic design. I'm scared, but I have to trust him; otherwise, I'll never make it.

JANUARY 10, 2014

I entrusted my manuscript to my father.

For four months now, I've been working on my book, on my roots. I think about it every day, often even at night: How will he react to my writing if I go all the way and decide to publish? How can I find myself without losing him? How can I dare to speak without hurting him? How can I be both myself and a part of him?

We spent the morning together. He was so happy to dress up nicely and have me go shopping with him, something we'd never done before. Mom used to oversee our wardrobes and was the sole authority on the matter.

Over lunch, I gathered my courage and spoke to him about *Momig*, the approach, the choice of name, the work of turning intimate texts into a book. He asked me the one question that mattered:

- "What can I do for you?"
- "Read the book, Dad, and welcome it as it is."

All afternoon, I waited to hear from him, going nearly mad. I had decided to publish the book no matter the cost, but I desperately needed him to love it, for this book is simply a part of me.

When my partner came home from work, he found me in such a state of nervousness that we dashed off to the movies. Upon leaving the theater, I had still heard nothing.

- "Let's go get a drink."
- "I don't feel like it; I'd rather go home.

   In truth, my heart was tight, and I felt cold, very cold."

   We drove in silence until my father's text arrived:

- "I read it straight through! It's remarkable!! Now I'm going to savor it!"

   And blood started flowing through my veins again.

Since the beginning of my work on *Momig*, I have thought of Otto Frank, Anne's father, who hid with his wife and daughters for two years in a cramped apartment, in fear and silence, without daylight, a warm meal, or a song.

We know the tragedy: the betrayal, the arrest, deportation to death camps in Germany, and this man, the sole survivor, returning one day to the door of that apartment, devastated. He had lost everything—his belongings, his wife, his daughters—and there he stood, in front of the door to his former refuge, his prison, his home, the place where everything was still possible.

It took infinite courage for him to open that door, to revisit that place, to breathe in its scent... Otto would find the diary his daughter Anne kept from June 1942 to August 1944. He would devote himself to its publication, just as he devoted himself throughout his life to all his ventures: with an extreme determination to succeed.

Anne Frank's diary was published in 1947 and would go on to achieve worldwide acclaim.

Otto lived to the age of 90. At the threshold of his death, he would say that what marked him most in his life was discovering how little we truly know those we live with, even after 730 days locked away together.

Otto finally met Anne, and for me, that is what truly matters.

FEBRUARY 10, 2014

You write, and your life becomes something else. Don't think about what you'll write tomorrow; don't reread what you penned yesterday. Write here and now, while it's fresh. Write the gesture, write the emotion, write your reality.

Recently, I began leading a circle of circles: Each person orbits their own center of gravity and joins in a larger movement that seems to have its own life, its inertia, its trajectory.

Momig is born through my words thanks to Jean-Pierre's energy, Hovhannès' kindness, and Vincent's wild creativity: I am their muse, and they dance around me.

There is something solar-system-like in our configuration, something greater than us that transcends each of us individually and in our collective whole. We are mostly at the stage of synthesis, but in this circle of circles, I sense an immanent synthesis, something that must be, a connection that surpasses us.

I need time, I need calm, I need to move forward step by step, and in doing so, I get there—where? It doesn't matter; the step is the entire journey. Everything could stop at any moment without leaving me feeling deprived or frustrated. I will simply have arrived safely.

FEBRUARY 14, 2014

In her printing shop, Adeline takes care of beings made of flesh and paper alike. She looks with curiosity at each manuscript that crosses her screen, whether self-published or from a major publisher, whether the result of a sudden impulse or a life's work. It arrives, simply, one day. And in her eyes, it will be treated like all its peers—with kindness and clarity, through the professional gaze of someone who learned on the job. Curious, playful, she reads it, gently correcting typos—"There are always some; it's strange"—making it her own enough to suggest, "Maybe you could...?" or "It might be better to...?"

But she can't help it; she loves beautiful things, harmony, well-done work. So, quietly—since it's not her role, nor what's expected of her—she blushes and whispers to me, "I love your book; it's magnificent. I didn't find a single mistake, which is so rare."

In her expert hands, the book takes on a whole new form: scattered, spread out in thousands of petals, heads up, heads down, heads mixed on large sheets of paper. The book no longer exists; the red thread is broken. Nobody after her will know what it looks like. She prepares the feast for the ogre waiting behind the glass wall—the ogre with a hundred mouths that will endlessly swallow and spit out cyan, yellow, magenta, and black, subtly blended to form o's and a's, strokes and curves, flesh and shadow.

Everyone waits for it: the colorist, the cutter, the folder, the binder, each person awaiting the mark Adeline has left for them, their cue, how to work quickly and precisely, to finish well and return home with the conviction of a job well done.

Everyone waits behind the glass, amidst the deafening noise of the presses, the heat of the dryers, the persistent smell of ink, the microdust filling the air, where it never stops, day and night, "Do you know how much an hour on these machines costs?"

I don't listen; I just try to breathe in small sips, amidst the deafening noise, focused on the proofs. I want Hovhannès' paintings to be true to his works. I want the lines sharp, the contrasts right, the softness palpable.

I want the smell of the ink to go away. I want the noise of the machines to cease. I want everyone involved in this project to feel like they belong to my family. I want to someday dedicate a copy of my book to each of them—each of them who, without realizing it, contributed in their respective compartments, caring for the next, polishing something from the previous one, focused on their craft, unaware of the expected outcome, my impatience, my concern, my desire.

FEBRUARY 28, 2014

I'm waiting for *Momig*.

It's my first, my very first; everything feels so new. I've already broken the waters. For months, tears spring forth at a mere phrase, a scent, a thought. I feel like a fountain, an inexhaustible source, everything flowing through my eyes.

I'm waiting for *Momig*.

I didn't want to wait for the delivery trucks; I'm hiding in my home's heart. Suddenly, the phone rings: "It's beautiful!" It's the team in Paris, congratulating me. The pallet was quickly stored, *Momig* is safe and sound, warm and dry.

I'm waiting for *Momig*.

Hovhannès, impatient, arrives, hiding a book under his coat to protect it from the downpour blessing this birth. I feel faint. I finally see it in real life. I hold it in my hands, all blue, smooth, soft. I wanted it to be beautiful and it's magnificent.

I'm waiting for *Momig*.

Hovhannès paces like a caged lion. He, too, awaited this book, which speaks of him, his paintings, subtly portraying his artist's life through my words, a life chained to his easel, free from everything else.

I'm waiting for *Momig*.

I make all the calls I'd planned but hadn't dared make because now it exists. I'm holding one in my hand. Even if it's just this once, I'll call and say I made it. The magic is working, and each person on the other end says, "Yes, come show it to us."

Momig has arrived.

It can all begin.

Barev, yes em.

Hello, it's me.

The soul sometimes sighs so deeply that it awakens the body.

– Mathilde of Magdeburg, a 13th-century Beguine

Stephen and Cécile Baudin

MIRROR OF TWO METAMORPHOSES

Stephen Baudin's therapeutic journey is far from being conventional; rather, it follows a dreamlike thread. Initially, he studied dreams, exploring their extensions and their connections to the waking world under the guidance of Roger Zanoni. This foundation laid the groundwork for his ongoing development, continuing in the company of Mr. Zanoni since 1992. His interest then turned to metaphysics, which he studied with two erudite former students of Maurice Guinguand.

Simultaneously, he delved into Taoist Chinese medicine with one of the pioneers of integrating biological decoding into acupuncture, Mr. René Zeender. In 2000, he graduated from the Zhao Bichen Institute as an acupuncturist. He opened his practice and then, in 2004, traveled to the Ladakh plateaus to study Amchi medicine with Chief Amchi Phumtsok. In Ladakh, he encountered a terma (hidden teaching by Padmasambhava) that he stabilized under the guidance of His Holiness Ogyen Trinlé Dorjé, the 17th Karmapa, on the 17th day. He entered a year-long meditation and, following the advice of His Holiness, began teaching this terma, swiftly intertwining it with his teachings on Chinese medicine.

Starting in 2010, he engaged in therapeutic follow-up with patients of Dr. Philippe Lagarde. The latter taught him the Heitan-Lagarde test for monitoring cancer rebound effects in patients. In 2013, he settled in Switzerland and founded the Ling Dao Center, which offers various courses, including a federal curriculum in Chinese medicine.

www.centrelingdao.ch

Cécile Taric-Baudin is a therapist and a yoga and meditation teacher. Transitioning from a professional dancer to a consultant in new technologies, she embarked on an initiatory journey around the world with a backpack, an experience that transformed her perspective on existence and way of life. For over fifteen years, she wandered the globe seeking medicinal and spiritual teachings at their source, living with masters, healers, and yogis in countries such as Guatemala, Mexico, India, and Nepal. It was in Thailand that she began training in energetic medicines, then she followed the path of the Maya and studied shamanism in Central America under Don Lauro de la Cruz. The understanding of the Self through energy captivates her and leads her to specialize in secret Tibetan yogas.

She intensely practices the path of awakening, with years of solitary yoga retreats (including the Six Yogas of Naropa) and meditation guided by her Geshe Lobsang Choephel. From a young age, Cécile was convinced that the universe is energy and that the energetic power inherent in every being constitutes an unlimited source of healing.

Today, she shares her knowledge and supports those who suffer or seek to evolve in their self-understanding and inner motivations. In 2021, she opened her center in Switzerland, offering individual consultations while organizing workshops, retreats, and training in energy healing, yoga, and meditation.

www.ceciletaric.org

Stephen and Cécile Baudin

MIRROR OF TWO METAMORPHOSES

The union of our texts into a single chapter reflects the essence of our relationship. Today, we walk this path together, but we have realized that even before we met each other, our personal journeys had been marked by similarities and synchronicities. Every time one of us experiences something, the other, unknowingly, often goes through a mirrored experience.

Thus, the idea of writing together became obvious—a result of our shared understanding of what metamorphosis means.

Stephen was literally struck by lightning, while Cécile defied the laws of nature through shamanism and healing energy.

We are delighted to invite you to share this chapter of our lives with us!

Cécile & Stephen

Stephen Baudin

FIRE FROM THE SKY...
WITNESS TO
A METAMORPHOSIS

It is only in the darkness of our own eyes that we get lost.

– Heȟáka Sápa

What a pivotal moment the tender period of adolescence is, with its paradoxes and grand flights of theories, punctuated by hormonal surges that crash into lazy abysses. I remember using my father's withdrawal from our family home as an alibi for my bad faith and my impulses to break everything. At 16, I was the strongest in the world—or so I thought—paired with the frustration of not being in control in this adult world which was blind and deaf to my presence. The ideas were there, but the means eluded me!

Looking back on my fifty years of life experience, I realize that adolescence follows a relevant thread that is woven into the macramé of our ancestors' fears. And yet, it is Familia that catches up with us at full gallop, adorned with its transgenerational patterns, with a uniquely vexing tendency to repeatedly confront us with our own conditioning. I entered this introduction to adult life with the natural presumption of either unquestioningly following or rebelliously diverging from these hereditary patterns. Like a puppet trying to lengthen the strings of its control in the eyes of its puppeteers, driven by a mere desire for emancipation.

KRAKOOM...

A translucent, bluish sphere, a metamorphosis of lightning, enters my home. It appears before my eyes, spinning in all directions in front of my kitchen. I am concerned that it won't head toward the open window opposite its entry point, as one might expect in such cases. Instead, it settles like an observer, resolute in not leaving this closed space with me in it. Then, without warning, the bluish sphere finds refuge beneath my heart, without any jolts or violence. The sensation of the sphere settling under my vital organ plunges me into a frightening paralysis! At this stage, I feel torn between the feeling of being in a bad dream with perfectly credible illusions and the active memory of the sphere within my body. My thoughts quickly jump to the prospect of a long and harrowing paranoia in the years to come.

Despite everything, I grow accustomed to the blue sphere tenant in my daily life, though it's not every day one is literally struck by lightning—or at least its avatar! These spheres, mostly known thanks to Hergé's *The Seven Crystal Balls*[1], are quite rare. But when one decides to visit the inside of your body, it's a whole other story!!! My mother, in a characteristic off-topic comment reflecting her lack of engagement, told me: "History always repeats itself!".

As for me, I start to engage in an epic relationship, strewn with strange perceptions and a disorienting magnetism. Here we are, the two of us, as if I were a child forming a relationship with an imaginary friend, something I had never imagined happening. That said, at this point, I have no intention of slipping into schizophrenia to make this cohabitation possible. I'm at home, and I fully intend to stay!

At the same time, this electroshock changes my vision of the world. My focus is no longer on understanding myself but on observing a certain familiarity that develops over the days with the sphere. No uncle, cousin, or even friend knows of or has experienced a lightning encounter like this. Time passes, and I develop an unconditional respect for the forces of nature, a foundation for a maturity that distances me from the existential considerations of adult life.

---

[1] In this Tintin comic, Professor Calculus (Professeur Tournesol) falls victim to ball lightning: an iconic sequence from *The Seven Crystal Balls* unfolds during an evening at Professor Bergamotte's house, where a storm breaks out. A luminous sphere, resembling ball lightning, enters through the chimney and causes the disappearance of the mummy. We see Professor Calculus hurled, along with his chair, onto the table, swept away in a whirlwind.

Until recently, I sought a mystical explanation for this lightning's intervention in my body. I expended phenomenal energy to match the cognitive level of the perceptions that constantly traversed me, all while being unable to give the sphere a face or any anthropomorphic qualities to befriend. I thus lived in a grand analogical theater with mystical overtones.

The paradox is that freedom appears when one has their feet on the ground and their head in the stars. One without the other is like a life spent struggling without being able to embody it. One cannot be wise without touching the earth, and one cannot stop being a victim without observing the flow of life as it unfolds outside oneself. My detachment from transgenerational patterns allowed me great inner creativity, intertwined with a profound solitude in being unable to truly share my life as tradition dictates in the great human tribe. I shaped myself this way, pushing the paradox to its peak until the dawn of my 50th year. My persona carried the fruits of past experiences like Santa Claus's large sack, the bottom of which was an energetic abyss.

My life oscillated between divorces and the births of my children, leading me to wonder if my confidence in detaching from my transgenerational patterns hadn't solved everything after all.

One morning, as usual, I went to narrate a dream to a great man dear to my existence: Mr. Roger Zanoni. After analyzing my dream, he explained that my mystical understanding of the divine thread of lightning in my body and my need to formulate a pseudo life mission around this event was misguided, leaving me, as always, to reflect.

In the days that followed, I came to realize internally that this lightning was merely a delivery of light to the energy already stored within me since birth. It was up to me to do with it as I saw fit.

Since then, my life has truly changed—a real metamorphosis. I no longer confuse the story of my life with my spiritual path; these two aspects are free and resist nothing within each other, as they do not belong to the same sphere of understanding. This "controlled madness" is in constant search of balance with my psyche but no longer demands any energy from me to comprehend my perceptions. It is a madness conducive to dreamlike metamorphoses, sovereign in its joy of experiencing the extensions of these changes at every moment.

My conclusion is that change exists within the psyche; however, the butterfly does not live within the caterpillar. Rather their perceptions are mutually transferred throughout the course of their brief passage on Earth.

Cécile Baudin

FROM THE ABYSS TO THE SKY

The mind searches, and it is the heart that finds.

— George Sand

THE GREAT LEAP

Hello, Earth

Ring... The bell indicates we've reached 4,000 meters. The airplane door opens, and the air rushes in without warning, invading the cockpit. The moment of the great leap has arrived…

I say one last prayer to the angels and all those in the realm of the unseen. *May your will be carried out!* An intangible force propels my legs, my heart beating to the rhythm of a pulsating faith. I sit on the edge of the abyss, my back turned to the outside. Armed with an instructor and a parachute strapped to my back, I dive into the great void. Sky-Earth, Sky-Earth—after a

30

series of aerial flips, my stomach flips before my body stabilizes in the posture of a space spider. I hurtle toward the ground at over 200 km/h.

Upon landing, I know it. My life will never be the same again. Just before boarding the plane, my life had appeared to me in different, intertwined scenes, like a giant puzzle searching for its central piccc.

Overflowing with energy and emotions from all sides, I focus on using the tip of my finger to dial my phone: *"Hello, Dad? Guess what? I just threw myself out of a plane at 4,000 meters! And guess what else? I'm going to travel the world!"*

The Loss of Meaning

It was depression that pushed me to accept this improbable adventure of a parachute jump. I was once again questioning everything. For more than ten years, I had shaped the art of dance through the grace of the body and the fluidity of movement. Then, sensing that my mind needed to prove itself in a world consumed by the race for productivity and material wealth, I embarked on new studies in marketing and successfully transitioned into the then-emerging world of the Internet. Demonstrating my abilities in both artistic and economic domains, I proved to myself that I *COULD*—pure and simple. But challenges of the body and mind, as well as worldly successes, were no longer enough to sustain me. Now, it was my spirit that was starving, struggling with unanswerable existential questions.

Fear in My Gut

I feel fear in my gut. It arises from nowhere, responding to no external threat. I know it well—especially from adolescence. It had crept in alongside my openness to others and to love. It feeds on my doubts and lack of confidence, thriving on my fears of both failure and success. My mind relentlessly ruminates and regurgitates unsettling, indigestible, or unresolved conversations at an overwhelming pace. Compulsive and negative thoughts seem to reign in my mind like merciless masters of domination.

After a few years of respite in a relationship I had ended, the infernal machine started up again.

My mind once again became my greatest enemy in the face of silence and the absence of the other. Hunger and thirst, overindulgence in food, and the impossibility of satisfying this inner beast that is never appeased by any amount of sweetness. Once more, I gave in to its destructive cravings, its insatiable and nauseating need for food. I collided with the limits of my body, with the capacity of my stomach to keep deep down and flat what I had so quickly shoved into it. Thoughts raced, jostled, and seemed easier to process through the grinding of my jaws and overly sweet drinks.

I burst into tears, screaming as I pounded on my mattress. There seemed to be no way out; eating and purging appeared to be the only way to ease this screaming tension in my gut. How many times have I succumbed to it, and how many more times must I resist for this cruel cycle of filling to cease? The last three years of my relationship had only put on pause what had tormented me since adolescence. I understood it as temporary emotional equilibrium, compensation for the kindness brought on by a romantic relationship.

Today, I needed to go further. I had to find, beyond external support, the true causes of this visceral fear. I refused to consider specialized clinics. No one in my circle knew about my crises. I didn't believe in medication; I saw it as just another potential addiction. Deep down, I knew the cause of my distress had nothing to do with food—it lay elsewhere. I would find it, and I would heal myself, without a white coat, in total freedom.

It was undoubtedly this ability to embrace freedom that the parachute jump had triggered. I decided to dare to open myself to the world. I didn't know how, I had no idea, but it would save me—it was my only way out.

THE QUEST

Preparations

Over breakfast, my itinerary took shape like small red flags pinned to a world map stuck on the wall. Plan a little but not everything. Decide only on the main stops, leaving the journey on the ground open to surprises that could only freely unfold when the obligation to go here or there was let go. Leave room for improbable encounters and all kinds of unexpected deviations. Plan, yes, but not too much, so as to avoid pre-conditioning this time which I wanted to fall outside the field of my current imagination.

My backpack had to weigh no more than ten kilos, preferably eight. That was the limit I set for myself—manageable for my shoulders and adaptable for added weight along the way. I meticulously packed and filled it as my new home.

What to Do in Kathmandu?

Excerpt from my journal, Kathmandu, Nepal:

"The day of Vipassana has arrived. I feel like I'm back at school during exam season, my stomach tight with apprehension and the excitement to do well. My mind is already fighting to convince me that this isn't self-inflicted masochism. I'm afraid this might be one of the hardest experiences of my life. All my vices are already castrated in advance by strict rules. Impatience, cigarettes, food… Should I tell myself I'm entering a hospital?"

Eleven hours of meditation a day for ten days. That's how the initiation to Vipassana meditation (meaning "to see things as they are" in Sanskrit) is structured, according to the teachings of Sri Goenka. It's a true surgery of the mind.

The essential instruction for the first three days, 33 hours of meditation, is to continuously observe the sensations of the breath in the small triangle below the nostrils. The primary goal is to calm the mind to make it more available and pliable. It's a power wash of the mind. But before the thoughts are scrubbed away, as I attempt to keep my attention in this small triangle, my thoughts seem to intensify to bullet-train speed. Simply giving my mind an order turns it into a rebellious teenager doing absolutely everything to disobey.

If only these thoughts had something intelligent or interesting to say. But no, they appear like a horde of hyperactive fleas, jumping anarchically and frenetically, only to inevitably land in the trash for their empty and often ridiculous content. I am disheartened by being disturbed by such nonsense when my true intention is to firmly maintain my focus on the sensations of my breath on the edges of my nostrils.

My mind tries to escape in a thousand ways: making me fantasize about the next meal, serving up tempting memories, reminding me to urgently recalculate my budget, dragging me into imagined or past conversations with loved ones and even strangers. Everything seems fair game for it to prove its existence and its mastery over me. This plays with my nerves and irritates me, adding a mountain of emotions to these uninvited ideas.

It's utterly demoralizing. I cannot maintain my focus for more than a few seconds. I vacillate between feeling swept away by invisible tornadoes and disappearing into a cottony, obscure heaviness. The worst of these feelings is coming back to myself—*from where?* I have no idea—after several minutes of unconsciousness, still seated but completely lost, outside space and time.

It's both impressive and exhausting. I feel like I'm rubbing shoulders with madness– my own madness.

This is where my battle lies. I've finally found the moment, the environment, and the teachings to face myself, something I've long sought.

On the 5th day, the sensations, more or less coarse, transform into a continuous flow of energy coursing through my body, from top to bottom and bottom to top.

I am no longer made of matter—I am pure, vibrant, luminous energy, with an electric blue glow in place of my spine. It's an intense experience, and I feel like I'm taking an elevator to another dimension. It's hard to say how long the journey lasts, long enough for me to return completely unburdened and filled with an indestructible faith born of this experience. I am transformed.

Fragments of a Journey to the Heart of Energy (Journal Excerpts)

Thus began the quest, which very quickly became, for many years, my very existence. The world, like a mirror, reflected the beauty, obstacles, and dangers of the inner paths to be traveled. Transformations cannot stand alone. They succeed each other, forming patterns like lace, infinitely multiplying. Healing through energy has become my new life.

Pai, Thailand

"I haven't fundamentally changed; I've gone further—exploring many different directions with an intensity that constantly shifts, requiring continuous adaptation to people, languages, cultures, environments, tourists, currencies, activities, moments of relaxation, and the search for what truly brings me joy. These elements have become indispensable in my life.

I've gone further in accepting perpetual change: frustration, tranquility, excitement, boredom...

Don't lose faith. Cultivate it. Every day. I am here, in my world. It is forming within me today. I transform every horizon into a unique ray of light before my eyes and all around me.

I no longer need to dislocate myself like death cutting out my past, examining what is strictly necessary and casting a wary eye on an unknown source of light.

Now, I focus on the vitality of my spine, my inner workings, and my body. I settle into my inner world and communicate with a sense of radiance and serenity. I allow myself to be guided, watching the universe while lying down with my head at rest, feeling the energy descend into me. I no longer search outside myself, on this Earth, for an equivalent to universal energy, its force, or its perfection. Instead, I call it into me and let it flow."

"Revelation: My power lies in my belly. I have overfed it, constricted it, and strangled it for years. By balancing this chakra, I now diffuse energy throughout my body. I had been able to offer this power in my relationships but keeping it entirely for myself had been impossible to manage. Until now, I had wanted to suppress it, deny it, and bury it in my flesh.

By accepting it, I can channel and direct it to fill me from within and endlessly radiate it outward. As it becomes stronger and more connected, I will allow it to flow freely without draining my own source."

San Cristobal de las Casas, Mexico

"Leave behind the mirror of the world and call upon the master. The master is the guide to the unknown and the guardian of the unknowable. The protector of the passage through little deaths—the necessary shedding that allows metamorphosis to occur."

THE MASTER

The sanctified master
The immaculate cross
I kneel at your feet
The breeze comes to caress me

Where is your people
Those of the subtle peaks
Those of the receptive abysses

May your power manifest
May your heart heal
I am both disciple and queen
Thank you for letting me follow your steps.

THE LITTLE DEATH

May the winds of life carry me
May the shadow before my door
Be swept away like a dead leaf

My memory, which I wish were boundless,
Is disturbed by childhood fears.
Searching for an ancestral treasure,
My cells will serve as the channel.

May gray turn to light
May the atom become a prayer
I dissolve into the void
And become dust once again.

The Essence of the Journey

Thousands of kilometers flown, driven, or walked, only to finally understand that the true journey is unburdened by any of these. The only barriers to manifesting our deepest desires are the narrow conceptions and limiting beliefs passed down from our ancestors, ingrained in our education, and reinforced by the perceptions we create of our surrounding society.

Yet, there is no healing without suffering. The mind is a creature of habit, and its conditioning can lead us to open and close endless loops of harmful, repetitive patterns. Today, I thank the emotional and mental turmoil that was decisive in my quest. It became the driving force that gave me the courage to take that first step toward freedom—the parachute jump that felt like a rebirth.

"Nowadays, I travel from my couch," as Roger Zanoni—Dream Master and renowned painter whom Stephen thankfully introduced me to—once said. The journey is, above all, internal. This realization, which all travelers eventually encounter, is perhaps one of the greatest lessons of the long road. Without it, the meaning given to the mere journey on external roads would quickly become futile and filled with a sorrowful fatality.

Through the takeoffs and landings, emotional fluctuations, and nervous digestion and integration, the flow of time changes shape. From linear progression, it becomes circular, unfolding into an ascending spiral where every moment becomes an opportunity to touch the infinite. The infinite of being—the extraordinary power to create life with every thought, every word, and every action.

"You descend with vision while you ascend with conduct. It is essential to practice these two movements as one," Padmasambhava, the second Buddha, teaches us.

The mind is unbound by any frontier. Reuniting within its space of limitless horizons reveals the grandeur of our true nature. Recognizing oneself in one's own light means embracing all beings within oneself—a self that can adopt all forms and fears none. This self, whose engine is the eternal power of love.

Magali Rochereau

THE VASTNESS OF AN UPSIDE-DOWN SKY

Magali Rochereau is forty-seven years old, with a husband, Philippe, and three sons, Jack, Louis, and Michel.

Magali has always been a Parisian and worked as a physiotherapist and osteopath until 2017 when she was diagnosed with breast cancer.

The upheaval of the illness made her reconsider the professional angle of her life, which represented a large part of her time. She allowed herself to shake up everything she had built up until then, to pursue her dream of radio, music, and voice.

She currently works at the microphone of France Inter and Fip, to her greatest delight.

Instagram: @acoupdepour.quoipodcast

Facebook: magali rochereau

Linkedin: magali rochereau

Podcast: https://podcast.ausha.co/magali-rochereau

Magali Rochereau

THE VASTNESS OF AN UPSIDE-DOWN SKY

One must have chaos within oneself to be able to give birth to a dancing star.

– Nietzsche

I realized my life dream: I am now a host at Radio France. I've finally become that woman I used to listen to on the radio, the one I imagined in the studio, paid to touch my soul through musical notes.

It's okay to choose the wrong career path, but for me, that wasn't the case. I feel like I was very passive, simply following what was presented to me among "practical" career options, without ever considering the person I am—my aspirations, strengths, needs, and tastes. The bitterness comes from the fact that when illness entered my life in 2017, I had already felt lost for a long time, condemned year after year to repeat the same motions, even though

I had enriched my physiotherapy practice with various additional training courses. I would count the minutes until the end of the day, craving the few vibrant hours that followed work, hours I tried to make the most of with far too many glasses of alcohol.

The question that haunted me was about the place I was meant to occupy in the world. Is it possible to become sick from not fulfilling one's mission on Earth? From not realizing oneself? Can the emptiness grow too vast? After going through the ordeal of cancer treatments, I created the podcast À Coups de Pour Quoi, a series of interviews with cancer survivors, centered around the question of "pour quoi"[2] (for what) in two words. I created this podcast to talk about life after this illness and its consequences, rather than focusing on the before and the causes—especially since the "why" of the illness often remains unknown. Could it be that such an internal conflict, about the place we occupy on this Earth, disrupts us so profoundly that it throws our bodies into imbalance, leading to the development of malignant cells?

In my case, the change was triggered by the onset of the disease. It was as if I had been waiting for it. "Something is going to happen," I thought to myself—and then it arrived, in my blood, in my breast, and settled there permanently. At first,

---

[2] In French, 'Pourquoi' in one word means *why*. Here there is a play of words by splitting "pourquoi" into two words. The meaning then becomes *'for what'*. "Pour" meaning *for* and "quoi" meaning *what*. The idea is to ask oneself, what was this cancer good for? How did it serve me now that I have some hindsight?

I took it lightly, convincing myself it would pass without much trouble. But when I received the same diagnosis a second time, my future became uncertain. This time, there was no doubt— I was at a crossroads, forced to find a way out in order to live, and thus transform myself. The life I had been living contained the seeds of something lethal.

Initially, I focused on improving my diet, striving to regain mindfulness, and committing to regular physical activity.

Then came the second step to climb. I had to understand the conflicts unfolding between those who shared my life and me: engage in deep conversations with my husband, reveal to him the pain some of his choices had caused me; speak with my mother to try to uncover the hidden shadows passed down from generation to generation; and, finally, confront myself—through the guidance of numerous therapists, each one helping me become aware of who I truly am.

The illness and the grueling treatments taught me to see myself differently: I became a woman who was suffering and exhausted, with no hair, a bare gaze, and one breast. The mirror revealed my deep vulnerability, and from it, I gained infinite strength. The more diminished I appeared, the more I began to feel a sense of respect for myself.

And from there, the climb continued with tests in the dynamics of life. I tackled the existential question: What have I come to do on this Earth? I cry as I write this—I want to heal from this illness so I can dedicate myself to making the world a better place.

At that moment, it became clear that the professional role I occupied was no longer aligned with who I was. Through a career assessment, I sought to understand the direction I wanted to take in my work. The answer was within me: radio. But it took me six months to articulate it, and when I finally did, standing in front of the career counselor, her approving gaze was decisive. Her encouragement gave this new path permission to exist.

From then on, my journey became fluid: attending the open house at the National Audiovisual Institute (Institut National de l'Audiovisuel), which offered the perfect training course; passing the entrance exam; obtaining the diploma; and receiving my first offers to host programs on regional stations. Once I was "professionalized," my task was to convince influential figures of my ability to work closer to home, in Paris, within the round house of my dreams, and persuade them to help me build the bridges that would allow me to reach my destination. Time slowed down as my diligent internet research led me to the right internship opportunities, and my perseverance and determination gradually wove the connections that brought me closer, month after month, to my new mission.

When I think back to the woman I was—lost in self-disgust—I feel immense compassion and deep love for her. I wish I could show up one evening at the door of her practice as her last patient of the day, ring the intercom, and tell her about the great adventure lying dormant within her. I imagine the dialogue that the woman I've become would have with the woman I once was: An imaginary conversation between me today, the "radio woman," and me yesterday, the "physiotherapist woman."

Radio Woman:

- Did you make it on time this morning? Was your patient waiting for you at the door? Did you push through, starving, without a break until 2 p.m., with just a tiny salad to stave off dizziness? Are you still fitting into your jeans? Did you wear heels? Can anyone see your gray hairs? You didn't see daylight from morning until night, did you? Do you feel like screaming? Do you hate everyone? Are you counting the minutes from the start of each session, repeating the exact same motions, even to the point of accidentally addressing your friends formally when you treat them because you can't break out of the routine? What's your joy today? Spending money at Petit Bateau between appointments? Did you treat yourself to a sandwich and a Coke? Did you make it through the day without crying?

- ...

- I wish I could take you in my arms, look into your beautiful, clear eyes, run my hand through your hair, and tell you not to worry about missing out on your full retirement. Because all of this—the grind—will stop forever. I want to see your face, feel your heart beat a little faster under that impeccable white coat.

Physiotherapist Woman, with a faint smile:

- What? Forever?

Radio Woman:

- You'd say, "That's scary," and I'd reply, "Yes, it's a steep price to pay, but it's necessary, Magali. You can see you're not getting out of this on your own." You're so miserable that I believe, even if you held the cards of fate in your hand and the terms were clear—Magali, your life would hang by a thread for the rest of your days; you'd never be sure if you'd still be here next year; you'd live dependent on medication that would age you too quickly—and you'd still sign.

- ...

- It's cancer that you've taken under your arm—and not just any cancer. From the outset, it's metastatic, far too advanced by the time it was discovered. It had to be this way. We'd probably go have a glass of slightly cloudy white wine across the street from your office. I'd sit next to you, keeping my hand on your arm, my eyes locked with yours. Maybe, after wetting your lips, your hand would tremble a little as you set down the glass, and you'd begin by wanting reassurance.

Physiotherapist Woman:

- I'll never come back here again? I'll never do this job again—ever?

Radio Woman:

- And you would add mischievously: "Is there something else waiting for me?"

  I'd say yes, and you'd realize it's not life that's ending. No, it's a second chance—the most beautiful gift wrapped in the stickiest, messiest paper. The chance to become who you are meant to be, and also the chance to keep those dearest to you close. You'd be excited.

Physiotherapist Woman:

- Okay, tell me more!

Radio Woman:

- You're going to know fear—the fear of dying. That's what will allow you to change everything: the cold breath on the back of your neck, the catheters, the transfusions, the IV drips, the stark awakenings in the middle of the night, the pale mornings filled with panic, the calculations and risky bets with fate, the looks you'll give your children, unsure you'll see them grow up, the nausea on test result days, the terror… And your new life will appear, day by day, hour by hour. Little by little, you'll allow yourself to believe in a different story, and at the same time, you'll begin to care for yourself. In the end, you'll love yourself.

You see, I'm touching you now, looking at you, loving you—and that will give you the strength to believe in yourself. That's all it ever was.

Physiotherapist Woman:

- And what's the gift?

Radio Woman:

- From where I'm speaking to you now, it's not over—it can go much further. So don't start limiting your beliefs. What's your dream?

Physiotherapist Woman:

- Wait, I'm feeling a little warm. I need something to drink. Tomorrow, like always, will be filled with pain, fatigue, and sadness. I have two healthy children, a loving husband, and a comfortable life, with nice vacations. So where does this constant dissatisfaction come from? This need to escape every evening with one glass, then two, then three, as long as we laugh and feel alive—just as long as something interesting finally happens! Otherwise, it's endless boredom; even with my overloaded schedule—work, kids to manage, groceries to shop for, invitations to accept or reciprocate—I'm bored, as if waiting for something to finally happen. This can't be all there is.

One day, a patient of mine had a reaction that struck me. At the end of her session, she looked at me intently and said, "You could do something else." I know that, but I'm drowning under the obligations of making ends meet, paying the bills to sustain this life that's slipping by inexorably. I can't even bear the thought of being in the same place when I retire. I'm teetering on the edge of an anxiety crisis; it's dangerous to keep waiting for an event that probably will never come.

My dream is to leave this dimly lit little room and do something other than touch the bodies of patients. I want to trade places with the girl speaking into the microphone on the radio I listen to all day long. I want to keep touching people—but with my voice.

Radio Woman:

- At that moment, you'll be like a child writing their Christmas list to Santa Claus, a naive smile on your lips, your gaze uncertain, knowing it's too much, that it's not going to happen, that the old man in red isn't a magician.

Now it's my turn to tell you about the moment when destiny bursts in—bold, shattering your life, but at the same time, opening up the possibility for escape. The turning point begins with a positive pregnancy test: Michel, the baby you sought out despite all reason, knowing three children is too many for you, and against your husband's initial wishes. The news of this pregnancy terrifies you, makes you doubt, makes you cry.

Michel, your third son, will unknowingly point a finger toward an infiltrating carcinoma that doctors failed to detect in your left breast despite their tests. After this pregnancy, the carcinoma appears—proud, massive, devouring the entire space of your breast and all the lymph nodes under your arm.

"It's a severe, extensive cancer."

This sentence will wake you in the night; it won't let you rest. It will consume you until the moment you decide to face it, to go beyond chemotherapy, mastectomy, radiotherapy, and hormone therapy. Your story is about exceeding the limits you've been given, realizing that the true light lies beyond the game you're being offered.

You'll remember Valérie, your patient who chose her own path against breast cancer. And so, you'll decide to call her. One dull February morning on Boulevard Bonne Nouvelle, she'll pick up your call and offer you her contacts—names of other therapists beyond the confines of Institut Curie. That's when the great adventure begins. You'll travel to Italy and Switzerland, returning with more bad news, gripped by fear, willing to do anything to get the treatments you need.

Another mastectomy. Along this winding path, you'll recognize your allies—those who have the important words. One day, you'll be ready to transform into the woman you are meant to be.

This journey will take you through a radio training program: entrance exams, a diploma, and then short contracts at France Bleu, where you'll grit your teeth through tears and pain. Thanks to this first job, France Inter will contact you, and your fantasy will begin to take shape in Paris. The following year, you'll apply for an internship at FIP, and your big dream will start to materialize. During that internship, you'll place the texture of your beautiful voice on their beloved pink microphone.

Today, from where I'm speaking to you, you have a regular contract at France Inter. And regularly, you climb to the seventh floor—your heaven—at FIP, with the promise that the next open position will be yours. You no longer heal the bodies of strangers, only those of your loved ones. And it makes you happy to keep that art in your hands, but it's no longer your job."

These words linger within me, like a truth that had been waiting for its time. I close my eyes and let the instant draw out, imprinting it in my memory. This room, this place where I gave so much, where I lost and found pieces of myself, now belongs to the past. I am no longer the one who wore that coat, who endlessly repeated the same gestures, the same smile, hiding the cracks that spread within. This body—my body—has weathered storms, carried the weight of transformation, and today, it is finally free.

I leave behind my past self, gently, quietly. A farewell without regret, just a whisper. The world outside welcomes me with a newfound freshness. The evening air wraps around me like a kind breath. Every step I take resonates like a promise, an invitation to move forward without fear, into the unknown. I walk with a light heart, and memories blend with the sounds of the city. I think of those days gone by—the exhaustion, the confinement. Of the time when I was just a shadow, a silhouette going through mechanical motions, trying to fill a void that nothing seemed able to soothe.

But life has its own path, its own rhythm. It shook me, forced me to open my eyes, to listen to that inner whisper telling me something had to change. I followed that whisper, despite the fear, despite the doubts. And today, I stand here, facing myself, ready to embrace this truth. This is no longer my profession, no. It is a garment I have left behind, a role I played for too long. Now, I stand bare before the future, with nothing but my voice, my breath, and a burning desire to touch the world in a different way. The wind brushes against my face, inviting me to breathe more deeply. The night stretches before me, infinite and full of mysteries. I no longer fear the unknown, for I carry within me the light that will guide me. This microphone, this dream that kept me standing, is only the beginning. A new page, still blank, awaits my words.

I look up to the sky, and the stars remind me that anything is possible, that life is vast, that the horizon is always further ahead. I walk, unhurried, each step in harmony with who I have become. Each breath is an homage to life, to my life, which I now shape according to my truth.

This path is mine, and I embrace it with the certainty that I am where I'm meant to be, at last.

Laetitia Garreau

WELLNESS DESTINATION

Laetitia Garreau is a wellness massage practitioner in Tahiti, specializing in ancestral techniques that promote healing and well-being.

Originally from Tahiti, she grew up on the island in a warm atmosphere surrounded by her parents and sisters, creating happy and joyful memories. After completing business school in mainland France, she chose to return to her native island to reconnect with her roots, build her life, and start a family.

Before fully dedicating herself to her passion for wellness massage, Laetitia explored various fields, including real estate—helping families build on their land—as well as marketing and sales. These experiences equipped her with valuable skills that she now integrates into her therapeutic practice. Through her commercial background, Laetitia has also developed attentive listening skills, enabling her to better understand the deep needs of the individuals she supports through her treatments.

A mother to a young daughter and in a committed relationship, Laetitia is on a journey of personal development that she cultivates for herself and for her clients.

Beyond providing relaxation and relief from certain physical discomforts, she views wellness massage as a powerful tool for reconnecting with the body, emotions, and sensations. For her, these treatments are valuable allies in nurturing the body, mind, and soul.

Laetitia firmly believes that every human being has the potential to heal and transform. This deep conviction guides her daily practice as she contributes to a more peaceful and harmonious world.

To discover the services offered by Laetitia:
Website: http://www.matariitahiti.com/
Facebook: Matarii - massages à Tahiti
Instagram: matarii_massages_tahiti

Laetitia Garreau

WELLNESS DESTINATION

For only to the extent to which people commit themselves to the

fulfillment of their life's meaning, to this extent they

also actualize themselves.

– Viktor Frankl

In 2019, while I was pregnant with my daughter, I happened to come across a video by Sarah Roubato on YouTube that caught my attention. In this video, Sarah shares her letter titled *"Find the Verb of Your Life: A Letter to a Teenager."* Through carefully chosen words, she encourages young people to identify what truly drives them, to find the verbs that inspire them to move forward, rather than focusing solely on choosing a "profession."

Although this video is aimed at teenagers seeking direction, its advice is relevant to all generations. For me, it sparked a reflection on how to give more meaning to my life and led me to rethink my career path. With the arrival of my baby, this reflection took on a more profound dimension.

My pregnancy was a genuine tsunami, and it wasn't just because of hormones. It went much deeper than that. I was very happy but bewildered at the same time. My interests had shifted, and I often felt sad, discouraged, tired, and irritable, all while grappling with intense guilt. It was a difficult period to navigate but it was also a positive one because it allowed me to rediscover myself.

THE DAY I BECAME A MOTHER

I was 32 years old when my daughter Temiki was born prematurely, after only seven months in the womb. She weighed 1.6 kg and measured 42 cm. She was immediately transferred to the Neonatal Intensive Care Unit at the hospital, where she stayed for four weeks. For her father and me, our new life as parents began amidst flickering screens, blaring alarms, and wires attached to her tiny body.

Very quickly, I felt immense guilt—the guilt of not being able to carry the pregnancy to term and the guilt of having to induce her birth to save myself. I also felt guilty for not delivering naturally but via cesarean section.

I remember the moment when the gynecologist told my partner and me that the situation was deteriorating and that he was preparing the operating room for an emergency C-section. My partner, sensing that our daughter would be born that day, had arrived at the hospital earlier than planned. He confidently said to me, "*She's fine, she's ready to join us.*" But *I* wasn't ready. I burst into tears. I was terrified at the thought of losing my baby.

My blood pressure was extremely high, and my organs were showing signs of damage. I had been hospitalized for two weeks in the high-risk pregnancy unit due to pre-eclampsia, a pregnancy complication that endangers both the mother and child. I had been warned that I would not carry to term and that the delivery would likely need to be an emergency C-section, though it was uncertain when that would happen. High blood pressure and the presence of protein in the urine are the main symptoms of pre-eclampsia, and the only treatment is delivering the baby.

I felt both anxious and hopeful. My hope was largely rooted in my trust in the medical care I was receiving and in the teams working in the high-risk pregnancy and neonatal intensive care units.

When I arrived in the operating room, the surgical team was waiting alongside the anesthesiologist. A few days earlier, we had discussed my health condition. He explained that due to my blood test results, if an emergency C-section became necessary, I would need to undergo general anesthesia rather than a spinal block.

I was very anxious about being put under anesthesia on the operating table. To help me manage my fears and stress related to the surgery, the anesthesiologist suggested self-hypnosis exercises. This was my first experience with hypnosis.

Everything moved quickly. I could hear the medical team preparing the equipment around me. I began to panic, but then I remembered the exercises I had practiced with the anesthesiologist. I managed to relax, enter a state of self-hypnosis, and visualize my safe space, while tuning out the noises around me. Thanks to self-hypnosis, I was able to handle the C-section with greater calm.

After the procedure, I wasn't able to see my daughter immediately as I had to remain bedridden for another 24 hours. My partner, who was with her in the neonatal intensive care unit, kept me updated and reassured me. When I finally saw Temiki for the first time in her incubator, so small with a large mask covering her face to help her breathe, I felt another wave of deep guilt hit me. She was connected to various tubes and wires. I whispered, *"My baby, I'm so sorry for what I put you through."*

Three days later, I was finally able to hold her skin-to-skin. The nurse gently placed her on me. I felt an immense love and an indescribable connection. In that moment, I truly felt like a mother, thanks to that physical contact. Her father also participated in this unique experience.

Over the next few days and weeks, thanks to the quality care and long hours of skin-to-skin contact with both her father and me, our baby's health improved. She felt secure, nestled in our arms. Her breathing stabilized, and the monitor alarms rang less frequently. She could feel our warmth, recognize our scents and voices, hear the beats of our hearts, and sense the softness of our skin. Additionally, she was being fed through a tube and the skin-to-skin contact helped her digest better. She regurgitated less and gained weight. These tender moments between her and us helped us all heal and grow stronger.

THE MEANINGFULNESS OF TOUCH

The precious cuddles I shared with my daughter made me realize just how much touch could influence her well-being and health. They weren't just comforting; they were essential to her survival and development.

The skin is the largest and heaviest organ in the human body, making touch the most important sense for humans. We can live without seeing, hearing, smelling, or speaking, but we cannot live without touching or being touched. It is, in fact, the first sense that a baby develops while in the womb and the last sense to fade before death. As we grow, this tactile contact, usually provided by parents, may diminish or even disappear, sometimes without any replacement. This is where massages find their meaning.

I remember an elderly woman I once massaged. Though she had received massages before, she burst into tears when she sat up from the table. I asked if she wanted to share her feelings with me. She then told me that her mother had passed away when she was a child, and the massage had brought back memories of her mother's nurturing embraces. She added that her husband, not being very tactile, rarely touched her.

This encounter reinforced my conviction about the importance of touch and massage. Massage is not just a relaxation technique or body care; it can also revive memories or fill an emotional void.

I became interested in massages when my daughter was a baby. The experience of her prematurity strengthened our bond to the point where, in the months following our discharge from the hospital, we continued with skin-to-skin contact, and I began to massage her intuitively. The massage brought her so much comfort that it became part of her bedtime ritual before falling asleep.

ALIGNING MY WORK WITH MY VALUES

When I returned from maternity leave, I felt out of sync with my job as a sales representative in a real estate development company. What bothered me was the focus placed on the company's financial goals rather than on client satisfaction.

What I valued most in my job was supporting my clients through one of the most significant steps of their lives. Owning a home is a dream for many, and buying a property or land to build on is often the most important purchase a person makes in their lifetime.

Guiding my clients through this process and having a lasting positive impact on their lives was what motivated me the most. There was nothing more rewarding for me than seeing the joy on a client's face after signing for their land or home.

Client satisfaction is crucial, not only for maintaining a good relationship but also for building a solid reputation. To me, people should always be the central focus in this job.

However, in the context I was working in, some of the company's commitments were not being upheld, which affected relationships and trust with some clients. This deeply troubled me, as the company's values no longer aligned with mine.

This feeling of dissatisfaction was heightened by my experience of motherhood and my time in the hospital. I needed to bring more meaning to my professional life and find a path that suited me better, though I did not yet know what I wanted or which direction to take.

This period was very uncomfortable for me. It eventually pushed me to resign from my position a few months later.

Fortunately, soon after, I found a job as a manager for two discount stores. It was a very enriching experience both professionally and personally. I was able to develop my management skills on both the administrative and commercial levels. On a human level, I had the responsibility of leading a team of six people. What I appreciated most in this role was infusing my team with positive energy throughout the day with the aim of achieving our sales goals. Together, we managed to create a pleasant and motivating atmosphere for everyone.

Unfortunately, the health crisis forced us to close down one of the stores due to a lack of supplies.

At the same time, my partner, who runs his own construction business, needed administrative support. He suggested that I join his team. I accepted out of love and because it felt natural to support him. We both knew, however, that this would be temporary.

INNER EXPLORATION

I have always been fascinated by the psychological aspects of relationships and human behavior, to the point where I once considered studying psychology when I was younger.

In 2014, during a difficult time in my life, a friend recommended a book: *You Can Heal Your Life* by Louise Hay. This book explores how beliefs, often rooted in childhood, can affect our body, mind, and life outcomes. It also discusses the process of change: how to initiate it, overcome resistance, and build a new world based on healthy, positive thoughts.

This book opened my eyes and introduced me to the field of personal development. I then sought out other books, watched videos, TEDx talks, and interviews on the topic.

In 2020, as I was reflecting on my career, I took a personal development course that uncovered a talent I didn't know I had. During a guided practice led by Sophie, I remember several participants noting that I had a "special sensitivity" in my hands. At the time, I didn't know that this sensitivity would guide me toward the world of wellness massages and eventually become my profession.

Meanwhile, I completed various training courses in hypnosis and self-hypnosis. My positive experience with the anesthesiologist in the hospital sparked my interest in further understanding this gentle method. Through this extraordinary tool, I had the chance to explore my inner world. During these explorations, I examined my values: those that guide my daily actions, those I don't like to compromise on, and those that, although secondary before, had become central in my life. This highlighted the importance of core values for me: love, respect, humanism, sharing, and tolerance.

TRANSITIONING TO A CAREER IN WELLNESS

I have always known that there are natural alternatives for self-care that complement conventional medicine. With my mother's Tahitian and Chinese heritage and my father's French background, I grew up in Tahiti, where Polynesian traditions, particularly ancestral care practices, were an integral part of my childhood.

When I was a child and had a sore throat, my mother would treat me with *Rā'au Tahiti*, remedies she prepared from local medicinal plants with recognized properties. I would use them as a gargle, and within a few days, my symptoms would subside. For muscle aches, she would massage me with *Mono'i* oil from Tahiti, which my grandmother carefully prepared.

These remedies (*Rā'au Tahiti*) and massages (*Taurumi*) are at the heart of traditional Polynesian medicine and continue to be an essential part of daily life for families striving to preserve this heritage.

In the past, only the *Tahua*—healers endowed with a gift inherited from their *Tupuna* (ancestors) and extensive knowledge of local medicinal plants—practiced these treatments, often accompanied by beliefs and prayers.

Rā'au Tahiti and *Taurumi* are much more than mere treatments; they embody a culture and expertise passed down through generations. Although my mother was not a healer, she firmly believed in these ancestral methods and learned them by observing the *Tahua* prepare their remedies.

I remember a story my mother told me about my grandmother, a story that convinced her of the efficacy of *Rā'au Tahiti*. Over 30 years ago, when my grandmother was diagnosed with lung cancer, doctors had lost all hope and had given her only a short time to live. My mother decided to take her to a *Tahua*. An elderly woman welcomed them into her home. Without saying a word, she observed my grandmother and then quickly prepared her remedy. She crushed plants in an *umete* (a wooden bowl) and made a decoction while murmuring words in Tahitian. She then gave my grandmother the *Rā'au Tahiti*, specifying the dosage and duration of the treatment.

A month later, my grandmother's cancer had disappeared. The doctors at the hospital were astonished—it was a true miracle!

My mother never spoke to them about the healer who had helped, likely out of modesty and because, at that time, Western doctors did not recognize traditional medicine. Today, attitudes have evolved, and more and more traditional practitioners are integrated into clinics and hospitals. My mother passed down this heritage to me. Massage became a natural choice for me, and the premature birth of my daughter strengthened my desire to deepen my understanding of the power of touch.

At the beginning of 2024, I began training in wellness professions to learn different massage techniques. At the end of this training course, I decided to embark on this path professionally by creating a massage company named *Matāri'i* (the Pleiades) to provide massage care in companies and at people's homes.

What I love about massage is the human dimension: approaching a person as a whole and being able to work on their physical body as well as their psychological and emotional state through caring touch, presence, and listening.

Listening, supporting, guiding, and accompanying each of my clients on their life journey is what motivates me. It's my guiding principle; "the verbs of my life."

As I write this chapter, it has been two months since I began my new wellness massage business. Although it does not yet generate significant income, I feel happy and fulfilled in my work.

A new path has opened before me, rich and exciting! I intend to follow it by continuing to learn and explore other wellness practices to enrich my approach and provide an even more beneficial experience to my clients.

To those reading this, I hope my experience can be a source of positive inspiration for you.

Pierre d'Alboy

FEAR OF THE VOID

Passionate about nature and human nature, Pierre d'Alboy was born in Senegal, where he grew up while traveling extensively, particularly in Asia and Africa.

With two decades of experience as a special education teacher, he has dedicated a part of his career to supporting children and adolescents facing difficulties.

In parallel, Pierre pursued an intensive practice in high-level sports and completed professional training in various outdoor activities, earning qualifications as a high-altitude mountain guide, ski instructor, as well as sailing and canoe-kayak instructor. These diverse experiences have enriched his skills and profile.

A certified coaching practitioner, Pierre spent ten years combining his dual professions, working both independently and in collaboration with human resources consulting firms, providing his expertise to companies.

As the founder and director of the association *T'Aider A*, he worked for five years to support children and adults affected by Attention Deficit Hyperactivity Disorder (ADHD).

Pierre continues to work as a tarot reader, numerologist, and coach, drawing from over thirty years of initiation, training, and professional practice in these fields.

Pierre d'Alboy

FEAR OF THE VOID

Know yourself, and you will know the universe.

— Socrates

To my daughter Amélie

My story is dedicated to the ugly ducklings, the restless souls, the brave cowards, the inveterate dreamers, the poets, the sad clowns, the budding artists, the conquerors of the useless, the stigmatized, the rejected, the abandoned, adventurers of all sorts, to all those for whom the path is steep but who nonetheless remain in love with Life in all its forms.

On June 10, 1944, four days after the D-Day landings in Normandy, an SS division called "Das Reich" moved toward the front and stopped in the village of Oradour-sur-Glane, about twenty kilometers from Limoges.

That afternoon, after gathering the entire population in the village square, these SS soldiers carried out a savage and violent massacre.

623 people—men, women, and children—were burned, shot, and executed. The men were killed in barns, while the women and children perished in the church. Only two survivors lived to tell the story of this massacre.

My uncle, Pierre d'Alboy, my father's beloved younger brother, was among the victims. And yet, nothing had predestined him to be in Oradour-sur-Glane that day.

After his train, which he was supposed to take from Limoges to return home, was canceled due to a bombing, a tragic twist of fate brought him to this village the day before, as a last-minute guest for a friend's engagement celebration.

He was 21 years old.

In mid-June 1974, I was 21 years old, bearing the same name as this uncle. An unconscious legacy passed down by my father in memory of his beloved brother, which would prove to be a heavy burden to carry.

I was driving on a road in the Vosges, heading toward Strasbourg, returning from a training course. On a straight stretch of road, I caused a spectacular accident and ended up trapped under a truck, miraculously between its two axles.

I had crashed head-on due to brake failure in my old 2CV. Immobilized and unable to move, I was pulled out of the wreckage by witnesses, while the truck driver hesitated to step out of his vehicle out of fear of the gruesome scene before him.

I emerged miraculously unscathed, with only a few scratches. And I resumed my journey as if nothing had happened, this time hitchhiking, a slight smile on my face—I had narrowly escaped death.

It was only much later, about twelve years down the line, that I made the connection between these two events. At that time, I had begun therapeutic work. I was trying, among other things, to understand why I felt compelled to roam the mountains, take risks, put myself in danger, and practice extreme sports—mountaineering, climbing, kayaking—without moderation, impulsively, and often alone.

I undertook some psychogenealogy work (see bibliography) with a therapist. This practice primarily involves gathering and compiling as much information as possible over three generations to construct a sort of family tree to visualize the family's history, the nature of the connections between its members, and significant dates and events.

In essence, the aim is to understand past actions in order to break free from repetitive cycles of events, as certain impactful occurrences in the lives of ancestors can resonate in the present generation.

This is where the concept of "synchronicity" (Carl Jung) comes in, which posits that two situations can exist without a causal link while being interconnected. These situations, occurring synchronously (within the same timeframe), share the same energetic imprint but manifest at different levels. Ultimately, it is the association of these two situations that gains meaning for the person perceiving them.

By connecting the two events mentioned earlier, I became aware of the emotional burden of bearing the name of a martyr who died for France (!) and the conditioning that resulted from it. In part, I found answers to my existential questions.

My guide then suggested that I undertake a sort of pilgrimage or symbolic action to help break free from the cycle of repetition and reclaim my own identity, distinct from that of my uncle. That is how I found myself one beautiful morning in front of the train station in Limoges. Arriving very early at dawn, I took the only available taxi and headed for the ruins of Oradour-sur-Glane (the destroyed village has been preserved as a memorial and a place for reflection).

Another sign confirmed to me that I was in the right place at the right time. Indeed, my taxi driver turned out to be one of the first people to enter the village after the tragedy. We exchanged emotional words about the purpose of my visit.

Very quickly, I found myself standing before the commemorative memorial where I could reflect in front of the plaque bearing the name of my uncle. It was an odd feeling to see my name on a memorial plaque.

It was a deeply emotional moment. I became acutely aware of the pain my father must have felt upon hearing of his brother's tragic death, especially when he had to recover the few charred remains of his brother's uniform and identity papers, which were used to identify him. In fact, very few of those who perished that day were identified and given a proper burial.

I realized that my father spoke very little about this tragic event. Sharing his thoughts and feelings within the family could have helped ease his suffering, liberate his awareness, and allow him to truly grieve while strengthening the bonds between us. For me, it would have provided the context of what he experienced and given me a better understanding of the close connection he had with his younger brother.

Knowing what motivated my father to give me his brother's name would have perhaps helped me cope better with its consequences. But what would have allowed me to heal the most, what I unconsciously longed for, would have been to hear that he loved me for myself and not as a shadow of his brother.

Nonetheless, I was there that day to fulfill a specific and symbolic mission: to clearly distinguish my life, as Pierre the son of Gabriel, from the life of Pierre the brother of Gabriel, which ended abruptly.

To do this, I retrieved all the relics that my father, not fully understanding the purpose of my actions, still had in his possession of his brother.

Once away from the ruins of the village, in a nearby field, I completed the symbolic act by burning these morbid remnants in a moment of reflection, with intention and great respect for this uncle I never knew, whose life was too short.

To conclude, I planted a stalk of wheat in the same spot as an ode to how life continues—a way of ending the conditioning and existing without this inheritance. Then I returned, simply and humbly, both happy to be alive and more conscious of the tragedy that had occurred here. I will never forget these intense moments.

Many years have passed, but I still look back fondly on this episode of my life. I can say that this experience, this awareness, saved my life. It prevented me from dying a hero or, at the very least, enabled me to survive.

This is why, after a long journey of personal growth and after working with and helping many athletes, mountaineers, executives, and business leaders, one observation stands out:

When we act compulsively and excessively in various domains, often driven by a near-morbid desire to push our limits, beware of danger.

Not knowing what drives us to such excesses—to endanger our lives and sometimes those of others, to burn ourselves out physically, mentally, and morally—is a warning sign.

In short, if we act without putting words to the deep roots of this agitation, the wall is not far off. It's an addiction, a conditioning.

At best, in work, sports, or art, this can be rewarding; at worst, in cases where it veers into alcohol, drugs, or smoking, it's far less amusing.

We risk missing out on the essentials—our physical and mental integrity, our relationships, our children, our family, our friends, our profession—life itself! In the end, we destroy ourselves from within, either abruptly or, at best, slowly over time, with the love of nature, effort, and sensations as our alibi. Because grounding our actions in a solid, understandable foundation increases our own safety and enhances our intuition (T. Ungerer).

KEYS FOR GROWTH

Personally, I delved into my family's past, did some introspection, sought help and guidance, pursued therapy, and explored various paths to better understand myself and act more consciously.

What saved me above all was meeting an exceptional woman who became my friend, my adoptive mother, my initiator—in short, my guide and mentor—for many years until her death.

She was a tarot reader, numerologist, and astrologer, but above all, she was authentic, attentive, discreet, dignified, and highly professional. In a word, she was genuine.

CONCLUSION

Don't hesitate to seek help and to remain open to new encounters.

In the same intuitive spirit, I began practicing yoga. I also needed to take care of my often-abused body and my restless mind. In short, I needed to finally find stillness. Breathing, meditation, concentration, flexibility, relaxation—not to mention the effort required to perform yoga postures—all contributed to my life balance.

My love for wild nature (a paternal inheritance and my main source of energy and life through my career as a mountain guide), my passion for outdoor sports, and my childhood, much of which was spent in Africa and Southeast Asia, greatly helped me transcend and exalt this hunger for activity.

In an extravagant way of reconnecting with myself, I opened several routes in high mountains (including a virgin peak in Pakistan) and on cliffs, and I soloed emblematic routes in Chamonix on prestigious peaks. Not to mention the countless times I exhausted myself in ski mountaineering races, cross-country skiing, marathons, triathlons, and more... but I already knew what I was chasing.

Another key factor in my understanding of life has been my work as a special educator. This role led me to work with many young people who were experiencing deep distress. Helping them had a mirror effect and greatly contributed to restoring my own identity (always staying one step ahead). By caring for them consciously, I was taking care of myself.

How could I not also mention the joy of being a father? At first, caught in the whirlwind of my hyperactive life, I felt helpless, overwhelmed, and on the verge of repeating family patterns. But gradually, I reached a form of maturity and did my best to embrace this paternal role.

I took my share of the transgenerational inheritance and reconnected with my parents.

To all of this I added a dose of creativity through painting, singing, and music to express buried emotions. I also maintained a good sense of humor to keep energy flowing and gain perspective, all of which was a solid and effective recipe for inner comfort and balance.

A BROADER REFLECTION

My personal story has opened my eyes to the depths of human beings in all their complexity. It invites reflection on the psyche (the conscious and unconscious manifestations of an individual's personality) and the benefits of self-work.

The origins of our ailments often lie in the wounds of our childhood, particularly early childhood (including conception, gestation, and birth). This is nothing extraordinary. The hardest part is identifying the conditioning and dependencies inherited from that time, which hinder our access to our true personality.

These issues arise from our adaptation—or over-adaptation (at the expense of our needs)—to our family, social, and educational environments, in response to traumatic situations and overwhelming emotions for which we were unprepared, defenseless, and unable to respond.

It takes great patience, time, energy, and courage to identify and release these conditionings and dependencies while staying fully alive.

The path is narrow for those who wish to learn to see, to shed their fears, doubts, and vain hopes, and to move from a child's consciousness (the past) to an adult's consciousness (the present). In a word, maturity means being an autonomous, respectable person.

Often, the trials we endure confront us with reality, acting as catalysts that push us to take action. Suffering alerts us to our shadows, urging us to understand and transcend them.

RELATIONSHIPS AS MIRRORS

A romantic relationship is an ideal space for growth but also for revealing our shortcomings, wounds, doubts, fears, illusions, and vain hopes. Without self-awareness and introspection, love can quickly turn to hate. Yet what a magical place to transform oneself, change beliefs, and gain a new perspective on love.

What a lesson in patience, humility, and acceptance—and what joy when we rise above, evolve, and help our partner do the same through sharing.

But without awareness of what is at play, the mirror effect takes over. We unconsciously seek our shadow in the other, pressing on their wounds while they press on ours. What conflicts lie ahead!

However, the path of a relationship offers a unique opportunity to grow, transform, and learn about oneself. Don't be afraid to seek help once again and progress at your own pace toward greater sharing, kindness, patience, understanding, and joy. Even the smallest possible step is always a step forward.

It is also comforting not to forget where we come from and to rejoice in the progress we've made.

FINAL THOUGHTS

Once the meaning of synchronicities is perceived, an immense field of exploration opens up—discoveries, shadow areas, and self-work. You won't stop being surprised by the roots of your suffering and the joy of being accompanied on this narrow path, leading to the liberation of your being.

On a personal note, I'll share this secret: It took me nearly four years of solitude—not entirely chosen, but fully embraced—to gradually undergo my true transformation.

Indeed, psychological time has little to do with Chronos, the god of time and passing hours.

Time, patience, and determination are integral parts of any profound change.

I will end with what I consider to be fundamental and essential: By opening yourself to a meditative and spiritual approach, which can simply be summarized as conscious breathing, you become alive.

Being connected to everything around us, rediscovering the heart's momentum, feeling the pulse of life, and appreciating the incredible fortune of being a human being, with its vast and largely untapped potential, is what is meant to drive us.

It's about creating even a small distance between ourselves and our body, ourselves and our mind, ourselves and our psychology, and becoming aware of our actions.

Close your eyes, breathe consciously and deeply, sit quietly for five minutes in silence, ideally in nature, doing nothing… relax, listen to your heart beating.

You are here.

POSTSCRIPT: WHY THE TITLE "FEAR OF THE VOID"?

Because I came into the world with a sensation of blankness, of emptiness, of abandonment, without a secure attachment bond to my mother.

My nervous restlessness, my frail and rickety appearance—expressions of suffering—were not understood, and I spent a large part of my life trying to fill this gaping void at the cost of colossal efforts to be seen, to be recognized, by doing everything possible to "be loved" despite it all.

Until the day I understood that my many photos standing atop dizzying peaks were really saying, "Mom, look at me." The connection between the mountain and the mother is very close.

Once I became aware of these false and vain hopes, the void took on its original meaning of fullness. The fear disappeared, and I began to love myself as I was, gradually opening my heart.

But that's another story…

APPENDIX

I would like to mention a therapeutic approach called PRI (Past Reality Integration- see bibliography), which suggests that we primarily suffer from our defense mechanisms. These mechanisms prevent us from feeling the unbearable reality of our past. This denial of the old reality is the cause of our emotional problems and the suffering we continue to experience (V. Beaufort).

This highlights the importance of being supported during self-work to reconnect with our internal resources and regain our creative power.

Another aspect that particularly resonates with me is neurodevelopmental disorders, more commonly known as ADHD (Attention Deficit Hyperactivity Disorder), which can cause behavioral issues.

This invisible disability, whose manifestations are sometimes mistaken for psychiatric disorders but which fundamentally stems from neuropsychology, can shed light on or even explain many otherwise inexplicable attitudes, situations, and behaviors.

BIBLIOGRAPHY: EXPLORING THE DEPTHS OF HUMAN CONNECTION AND SELF-DISCOVERY

Les Empreintes de l'Invisible by Tchalai

The Ancestor Syndrome by Anne Ancelin Schützenberger (on psychogenealogy)

My Brain Still Needs Glasses by Annick Vincent (ADHD for dummies!)

Se Libérer de la Blessure d'Abandon by Valérie Beaufort

Rediscovering the True Self by Ingeborg Bonomo (PRI therapeutic approach)

No Ordinary Moments by Dan Millman

This work draws inspiration from psychogenealogy, a therapeutic practice popularized by **Anne Ancelin Schützenberger** in her seminal book *The Ancestor Syndrome*. This approach emphasizes the lasting impact of ancestral trauma and explores how understanding our family history can free us from inherited emotional burdens.

The therapeutic model known as **Past Reality Integration (PRI)**, developed by **Ingeborg Bosch**, also features prominently in this journey. Bosch's book, *Rediscovering the True Self*, underscores the profound influence of early life experiences on our current emotional struggles and highlights the healing power of addressing deeply buried memories.

Similarly, the insights of **Valérie Beaufort** in *Se Libérer de la Blessure d'Abandon* emphasize the necessity of confronting our defense mechanisms to overcome the pain of abandonment.

The thread of personal transformation weaves through the works of **Dan Millman**, whose book *No Ordinary Moments* illuminates the spiritual and physical challenges we face on the path to self-actualization.

Another resource, **Annick Vincent's** *My Brain Still Needs Glasses*, provides clarity on ADHD, offering practical guidance and deeper understanding of this often-misunderstood neurodevelopmental condition.

Finally, I draw upon the poetic resonance of **Tchalai's** *Les Empreintes de l'Invisible*, which reflects on the hidden imprints of past experiences and their influence on our present lives.

Through these references, this bibliography integrates modern psychological theories and ancient spiritual practices, offering a rich tapestry of self-reflection, healing, and empowerment. It serves as a testament to the transformative potential of self-work, meditation, and the connections that define our human experience.

Fanny Clappier

DARE, DREAM, SHINE

My name is Fanny Clappier, I am 28 years old, and I am from Savoie in France.

I would describe myself as an entrepreneur passionate about digital communication and "human" marketing. With a Master's degree in Advertising Strategy and Digital Communication, I ventured into the entrepreneurial world straight after graduating by founding my own communication agency, *Alpine Com'*. For more than four years now, my goal has been to make a living from my passion while contributing, in my own way, to creating a better world.

I design websites for people who, like me, are passionate about their craft and want to turn it into their livelihood, as well as the entire graphic universe that comes with it. I draw all my ideas from

Mother Nature herself, who holds a central place in my life. I love to embrace my intuition and the messages from my heart in all my creations.

Along my journey, I have had the opportunity to train in various personal development practices and alternative medicine approaches. Certified in Naturopathy, NLP, RNCP Coaching, and more, I enjoy expanding my horizons and nurturing my curiosity.

Through my experiences and knowledge, I am deeply committed to supporting wellness entrepreneurs with a holistic approach that helps them thrive in their field. My "Business Coaching" program is built on three pillars: mindset, visibility, and well-being.

Website: www.alpinecom.fr
Support for wellness entrepreneurs: Business Coaching
Instagram: https://www.instagram.com/alpine_com/
Facebook: https://www.facebook.com/AlpineCom

Fanny Clappier

DARE, DREAM, SHINE

Osez, imaginez, brillez.
Dare, dream, shine.

− Fanny Clappier

These three words in French, one sentence, one quote, have carried me for years and contributed to my professional and personal success. This is what I would like to share with you through my story, hoping it will inspire you and give you the 'momentum' to change the course of your life.

When I was little, I wanted to be a veterinarian. I love animals, their unconditional love and innocence that make them both so strong and so vulnerable. Then, as I grew older, I was told that becoming a veterinarian required 'perseverance,' that the many years of studies needed were tough and long. Like many children, I simply abandoned this childhood dream to look for another career that would give me the same butterflies in my stomach. We are taught at school and in society in general that you have to work hard to earn a good living, that security lies in the salary you'll earn each month, and that studies are a passport to entering professional life. But we quickly understand that you have to be incredibly smart to succeed in higher education. Yes, we're not exactly helped along the way… Nevertheless, with entrepreneurial parents and not too many struggles at school, I decided to pursue a path that would become my passion today: communication and marketing. Five years of higher education, and I'm still learning to this day—thank you dear limiting beliefs who told me I wasn't cut out for higher education. Those five years, filled with studying, parties, new connections, internships, and introspection, taught me a crucial lesson that I still nurture every day as an entrepreneur: Our knowledge is a strength that becomes even more powerful when guided by a purpose. And for me, that purpose was to open my own communication agency. But before we get there, let's go back a few years ago… As a work-study student in a pharmaceutical group, I realized over the months that a deep need was slowly growing within me: the need for freedom. Despite the richness and learning experiences of those two years of work-study, I didn't feel like I was fully in my element. I felt trapped, drawn into an emotional whirlwind that was very uncomfortable for me. The tasks I carried out didn't provide the fulfillment I longed for… So, to fill this lack of freedom, I clung to the idea of promoting an alternative medicine that, for me, had real meaning.

Alone in my student apartment at night, I began to envision my future. What could truly make me come alive, where the words 'meaning' and 'freedom' would be at the heart of it all? I pictured myself as an independent, self-employed woman, free to set my own pace, to express my creativity in the way that suited me best, and above all, to listen to my heart, body, and intuition without this being labelled 'unacceptable' in the professional world. Yet, my own limiting beliefs kept whispering in my ear: 'It won't work. I won't be financially secure enough. I'm not good enough.' You get the picture—so many negative thoughts that were far from constructive as I approached the end of my studies.

When my work-study period came to an end, I faced a choice: accept a permanent job where this feeling of confinement would take up a lot of space, or go at it alone, be free, and strive for a passionate career in which I could create my own value and a business that reflected who I was. Unsurprisingly, you already know which option I chose. From that moment, a spark of creative inspiration began to grow in me. I felt like a child at Christmas, thrilled at the idea of discovering what awaited me. Starting my own business was the greatest gift I allowed myself to experience. I made space for my intuition and my heart, letting them guide my actions toward the right path, and I've never regretted that choice. On the first day of my business, I already had four clients signed on... And to think, I'd considered taking a part-time job 'since it usually takes three years to start fully living off a business.' Can you imagine?

Waking up whenever I want, organizing my days as I wish, working in nature if I feel like it, creating while following my intuition, and being the sole initiator of every action and decision I make, fully responsible for them all. As I write these lines, this has been my work pace for over four years now. My heart-centered career, as I like to call it, continues to grow each year.

But—there's always a but—a dark year made its way into my life. That year, I learned that my father was diagnosed with an advanced stage of cancer and I was scammed into a poor real estate investment, not to mention, of course, all the usual daily challenges... This situation brought significant changes to my life, which had an impact on my inner state of being: fears, anxieties, pressures, uncertainties, anger, injustices... A major drop in activity nearly forced me to close my agency, even though my communication strategy remained the same. Without ever truly knowing when it would all end, I experienced something incredible that helped me keep my head above water: The power of our mindset and inner well-being intimately influences the results we can achieve, both in our professional and personal lives.

My father's battle against cancer has been one of the greatest challenges of my life. My hero, the man I believed could overcome anything, suddenly became vulnerable. A career military man, my father has an iron will. A fighter and a rationalist by nature, he decided to take on this illness as a challenge and started hormone therapy based on the decision made by the doctors in his oncology department. He became a tremendous source of inspiration for me, as I was in the middle of studying naturopathy at that time. I had developed a passion for alternative medicine over the past few years, with naturopathy representing, in my opinion, a school of life. The synchronicities of the universe can be surprising, can't they? I decided to dive into supporting cancer patients, trying, at all costs, to help my father in his fight against this illness. Since I wasn't yet certified, I directed him toward practitioners who do incredible work for those who believe in it. This complementary path to conventional medicine, both psychological and physical, yielded results far beyond what we could have imagined. The doctors, who had been less than optimistic and had given my father only a few months to live, were quite surprised by the results. As I write these lines, no metastases are present in his body. I must not overlook those who have to deal with this terrible disease and do not experience a remarkable recovery, but let's keep our hopes high for the future of our story. This cancer gave my father the opportunity to change his relationship with his body, his lifestyle, and his way of thinking.

That same year, I invested in my future home. A project initially meant to bring security and pleasure, but as the months went by, it became the second biggest challenge of my life. After three visits to the house and a dozen others in between, I felt an inner calling. It was this house and no other. A few months earlier, I had crossed paths with the man with whom I share my life today—the one with whom I can laugh about anything, who brightens my days, loves me just as I am, and who supports me through every difficult moment—a man I admire and who makes my heart race. Just between you and me, these tough trials we were about to face together just a few months after meeting each other were anything but sexy…

So here we were, standing in front of this house to start the initial small-scale renovations we had planned when we bought it: moving the kitchen to another room, creating an opening to bring in more light, and updating the decor to our taste. I still remember the first day I swung my hammer to break down drywall. As the hours passed, our faces grew more and more disheartened. The house was filled with hidden flaws and shoddy work…

This project, which was initially supposed to take only a few months before we moved in, is still, to this day, a complete renovation from A to Z. Financially, things began to get very difficult. My mind was fixated on two questions: 'Will we be able to earn enough money to tackle the scale of this project? When will we be able to live in it?' Not to mention that we could only hire the bare minimum of workers to avoid going completely broke. So, we spent every weekend and holiday working on it, and three years later, the project is still not finished. That initial inner calling that felt so right, that immediate connection and vision I had, had turned into a real nightmare. At least, that's how I felt at the time.

At the same time, I decided to seek guidance to gain some perspective on the situation and try to find a bit of relief in this overwhelming storm. My coach, Claudia, told me two things that would change everything for me: 'Fanny, you are not the weather; you are the sky. Your security resides nowhere but within you.' It was true—I had been trying to solve the house problem with something external to me: a miracle solution, a court ruling, working even harder to earn more... I was letting my emotions consume all my inner space and deeply affect my way of being and living. I was wrong. The very first thing to do when a problem arises is to observe our thoughts and emotions around the circumstance. As Dr. Joe Dispenza's work has shown, our thoughts directly influence the outcomes we achieve in life. And here's proof of that:

We didn't know how we'd get through the financial strain caused by buying this house. With a mortgage to pay, all my thoughts were obsessively focused on the additional expenses we'd have to cover for the complete renovation of the house, and on the fact that I was self-employed and didn't have a very stable financial safety net. That little voice in my head kept repeating, 'I won't make it,' 'I'll have to take on a permanent job,' 'I'll have to sell this house at a loss...'

Since each of our thoughts generates emotions, we have the power to instantly create our state of being. For me, it was anxiety, stress, panic, anger, a deep sense of injustice... Not to mention the fear about my father's cancer, which was my biggest fear that year. But strangely enough, I handled that battle in a completely different way. I told myself that I had no choice—I had to find a solution to help my father win this life-or-death battle.

As a result of this state of being caused by our thoughts and emotions, we naturally take actions to achieve the results we want in our lives. The actions I was taking, however, stemmed from a place of very negative thoughts and emotions that did not serve my goal at all. I worked twice as hard, yet I wasn't really focused. I concentrated on useless tasks, didn't innovate, and stagnated. I juggled multiple projects simultaneously, and in moments of panic and anxiety, I tried a thousand and one things, thinking I could solve all my problems by doing so…

As you might guess, the results I achieved were far from satisfying. That year, my revenue was at its lowest. I was barely making enough to cover my mortgage and meet my basic needs. Thankfully, I had the support of my parents and partner, who stood by me during this challenging period.

With my story as an example, dear readers, I'd like to ask you to define the issue that obsesses you most and ask yourself: What are my thoughts and emotions around it, and what actions am I taking to move toward the outcome I most desire? You likely ask yourself what the right formula is. The winning formula is quite simple. By changing your thoughts, you'll change your emotions and, therefore, your state of being. You'll take actions that are far more relevant and effective, and life will handle the rest for you to reach your goal.

Believe me, I tried this method for months, and bingo, the following year, I literally doubled my revenue. I felt lighter, controlled my thoughts, and envisioned my future as if I were already living it. I won't pretend that all my worries have completely vanished from my mind, because let's be honest—I'm no Buddha. I still have a long way to go before feeling entirely at peace when I think about that house, but I chose to walk this path with immense gratitude.

By working on my thoughts and nurturing my inner world, things fell into place just when I needed them most. Instead of focusing on the problem, I shifted my thoughts toward the goal I wanted to achieve: to finance our home renovations and support my father in his fight as best I could.

The Universe, life, space, God, or however you name this energy we all dance with every moment of our lives, is essentially a game you play with yourself. Self-knowledge is the greatest gift you can give yourself.

Speaking of personal development, I want to thank all the people, therapists, and practitioners life has placed on my path who have helped me on this personal journey. Even today, I continue to work on myself, my thoughts, my emotions, my limiting beliefs, and my 'traumas' to make this life the most beautiful it can be. We never stop improving, learning, and growing. Our brains and souls are designed to experience and evolve endlessly.

After that dark year, a new aspect of my business emerged that aligned all my passions into one career: the 'business coaching program.' Passionate about communication, marketing, personal development, and alternative medicine, I asked myself: How could I combine all my passions into a single offering to help make this world a little better? The butterflies in my stomach returned. Perhaps this project will evolve someday? It is quite likely, but for now, I am committed to guiding the entrepreneurs that life brings my way, teaching them how to live from their passions and shine in their heart-centered career. I help them work on their mindset and state of being, without neglecting their visibility strategy, so they can thrive in their project through aligned and magnetic communication.

The takeaway from my story is this: Regardless of your goal, if you manage to elevate your thoughts and listen to your emotions and intuitions, you'll build something even more extraordinary than you could have ever imagined.

So, dear readers, what is that job, passion, project, or state of being that makes your soul come alive? What life do you want to live? Will you let yourself be ruled by your thoughts, or will you take charge of your life? A new chapter now opens before you, so dance with life and open the field of possibilities to make your journey even more passionate.

What if you Dared to Dream and Shine?

Achim Nowak

DEPARTURES

Achim Nowak is the author of four books on personal excellence, an Executive Coach, TEDx speaker, and host of the *MY FOURTH ACT* podcast.

Achim's writing has been recognized with a *PEN Syndicated Fiction Award*. He is a 2024 MacDowell Fellow, a 2024 Ucross Fellow, and he has been featured in *The New York Times*, *The Wall Street Journal*, *The Miami Herald*, *USA Today*, among others.

Achim is a citizen of the world. Born in Germany, he has lived in Portugal, Turkey, the United States, Trinidad and Tobago, and currently resides in Portugal again.

myfourthact.com
achimnowak.com

Achim Nowak

DEPARTURES

There is a voice that doesn't use words. Listen.

– Rumi

I sit at the dimly-lit bar of a cocktail lounge inside the Warwick Hotel, Sixth Avenue and 54th, Midtown Manhattan. May 1999, a late Tuesday afternoon.

My body tilts toward Carol, my conversation partner. Carol is an attractive woman in her 50s, her body impeccably poured into a grey pant suit, her demeanor polished yet casual, punctuated with an unforced smile.

Carol is the VP of Human Resources for a blue-chip Wall Street firm. I have just met Carol earlier that day. She is attending a training program delivered by my mentor, Herminio. I have been sitting in the back of the room, observing Herminio do his thing, taking notes, learning the program from him. It is my first week on the job.

Carol and I talk about this and that. Breezy bar chatter. Inconsequential. Until Carol declares: *I left Paris 7 years ago to move to Manhattan. I feel a change coming on. I believe in com-pletely changing my life every 7 years.*

On we banter. This, that. But my thoughts that night pivot back to the number 7. I have questions about this new job, don't know if it's what I should be doing with my life. How blissfully freeing Carol's comment is. I think she has just changed my life.

This is where I am, what I'm doing, now, today. Not forever. Now. Just now.

*****

I turn the corner of Commerce Street in Manhattan's West Village and head West on Barrow, in the direction of Hudson. It is a block lined with impeccably tended brownstones, mid-sized apartment dwellings, looking all pristine, movie-set Manhattan. This is my hood. An exquisite quiet hangs in these streets, on this mid-week morning, fall of 2003. None of the revelers who roam this neighborhood on weekends are out and about. Just the stillness. The calm. It lets the beauty of these buildings sing.

"I love it here," I think to myself, in that moment. Sometimes, insight is literal. This is one of those moments.

"What do you love about living here?" a voice in my head asks. When it's clear, it's clear. "I love the quiet, and I love being close to the water." Water, this morning, is the Hudson, 2 blocks away.

And then, the punchline.

"If you want quiet and the water, you don't need to be in Manhattan anymore."

*****

Miami, 1995. Another turn. I have just facilitated the first afternoon of a 3-day AIDS Mastery program at Mercy Hospital in Coconut Grove. Hugo, my host in whose North Beach apartment I will crash, picked me up at Miami International earlier in the day. Now, seated next to him in his battered Volkswagen Beetle, we zip past the high-rises of Brickell and the decaying Miami Downtown.

When we peel off Biscayne Boulevard and swing up to the MacArthur Causeway, the entire grand Miami panorama sweeps into view. The glistening waters of Biscayne Bay that refracture the sun. Tiny white bridges that lead to lush green islands in the bay. In the distance, the sun-kissed high-rises of South Beach. And the sky above, so tender and pale blue.

My heart bursts. Open. This requires no effort, no decision. An immediate sensation of joy washes over me. Big, wide, extravagant joy. I sense, in a way I cannot put into words just then, that the joy I feel is a joy that transcends this place. It is the joy of all my water views, in Tobago, in the Portugal of my childhood, water views of previous lives, all poured into this one sublime moment.

I don't think "hey, I want to live here." It isn't the time, just yet. Or perhaps it is, and I'm simply not listening.

*****

We know what we want, Tom Asacker asserts in Unwinding Want[3]. It rarely is what our thinking mind tells us we want.

You know that moving your body and being outside is better than being stationary and staying inside.
You know that doing things with people beats doing them alone, and that playing to play is more fun than playing to win.
And you know, and I know, that being all in or all out beats being half-assed or half-hearted.
We know all of that, but we may not know why.
Deep down we also know what we want.
But our thinking minds have blocked that natural flow of intelligence.
Because we're all wound up.
We know too much.

*****

Nine years after my initial MacArthur crossing, I am back in Florida. February 2004. Spend a week with Jose, a Miami colleague. Jose lives on the second floor of a quintessential Miami-modern apartment complex, wrapped around a courtyard, in the tony suburb of Coral Gables.

---

[3] Tom Asacker, *Unwinding Want: Using Your Mind to Escape Your Thoughts* (2024; independently published)

I rise early every morning, Jose still in deep sleep, and leave the apartment. Head for the corner of Ponce de Leon, hang a right, and make the long walk down to the Starbucks on Miracle Mile.

Ponce de Leon Boulevard at 7 is empty. I lean into the humid morning wind, the majesty of the palm trees, the brilliance of the morning light. This emptiness in which I can breathe.

I could live here. The thoughts come. *Maybe it's time to live here. Why not live here? It might be nice to live here. Yes, I could.*

And then I simply know. With every one of my senses. Know.

I don't do a mind-fuck.

Because when we know we know.

Fly to Miami once a month. Stay with Jose. Get a real estate agent in South Beach. Look at condos. Mid-beach. Normandy Village. Not sure. Spend a weekend in Ft. Lauderdale, No, not for me. "You would love Hollywood," those who know me say. Repeatedly. I stroll down the Hollywood Beach Broadwalk. Rough around the edges. Yes, yes. Walk into a real estate office. Gina and I look at condos on the beach. Nothing I love. Plop down some deposit money for a loft, preconstruction, Downtown Hollywood. Need to rent while I wait. Stroll down Harrison Street Downtown. Pass a sign. "All About Eve Media Services." Hhhmmm. That looks like a lesbian joint. I walk in. Yes, a lesbian joint. I tell Rose, one of the two eves, that I need an apartment. *Let me speak with my landlord*, Rose says. *There might be something where I live.*

Yes, there is.

Those are the tactics. Once we know, the actions are easy. The path is shown. It always is.

Six months after my week with Jose in Coral Gables, I move into my apartment in Hollywood, upstairs from Rose.

WHEN THE CALL TAKES US FAR AWAY

Sometimes life is a cliché. In my case, the cliché took me very, very far from everything I knew.

In the final week of 1988, I was diagnosed HIV+. My T-4 cell counts, then widely considered the key indicator of a person's immune health, were low and kept plummeting. Dr. Howard Grossman, my physician and a preeminent AIDS expert in Manhattan, sat me down in his basement office on East 29th Street. Expect to be in the hospital within two years, he announced with a somber voice and serious-doctor demeanor. That'll be the beginning of the end.

If you had only 2 years left to live your life, how would you live it?

The question IS a cliché. Well, I lived it. Took myself to a controversial healing center in the Arizona desert. 6 weeks, end of 1989. The Golden Phoenix promised that, through a combination of intense body purification and mental work, it would turn HIV-positives like me HIV-negative.

Toward the very end of my 6 weeks, Reverand Mona, the spiritual leader of the Golden Phoenix, took me on her version of a vision quest. Blindfolded me, confined me to a cot in my bedroom, to the thoughts and visions running through my mind.

I remained blindfolded for 2 and ½ days. On this cot, in my dark night of the soul, the visions came. Furiously, unsparingly. One, especially, came again and again. A white house perched on a cliff, high above the ocean. White house. Cliff. Ocean. Clear. Again, and again.

This much I knew when the blindfold came off: The white house wasn't a metaphor. It was a real house. The ocean was the Atlantic. The house was somewhere in the Caribbean. And I had to find it.

6 months later, I moved into a little white house, perched atop a set of boulders and rocks, on the remote island of Tobago.

Pretty wild, when I think about it now.

Before I found this house, I would not have been able to show you Tobago on a map. Island life can be expensive, and I wasn't wealthy, by any stretch of the imagination; I was living entirely hand-to-mouth.

When the vision is clear, the path is revealed.

I lived in my little white house for significant portions of 1990 and 1991. Became an accomplished windsurfer, among many other things. And when I was done, I knew I was done.

Yes, I went pretty far away. You have your own white house. Every one of us does. We go to great lengths to not see it. The beauty of Reverend Mona's intervention was that she forced me to see.

Don't wait. Notice.

*****

When I returned to Manhattan, 2 years after the first vision of my Tobago white house, the gifts multiplied.

I had not died just yet.

My blood work, all of it, was better than it was 2 years before I went to the islands.

Of course I could get another job, again.

Of course I could get health insurance, again.

Of course I could take care of myself, again.

Tobago showed me that I can depart. Go far, very far, leave it all behind, everything I thought I couldn't. Come back and start again.

I can. I can. I can.

DITCH THE BUCKET LIST ALREADY

July 2024. My partner David and I take possession of an apartment in the Fonte Nova neighborhood of Setubal, a commercial fishing port 40 minutes South of Lisbon.

It happens fast.

We have contemplated a return to Europe for several years. Amsterdam, perhaps. Or Duesseldorf, a city we love. In the spring of 2023, David and I spend some time in Lisbon. During this stay we take a day trip to Ericeira, a fishing village turned international surfer town, 45 minutes northwest of the city. When I was a young boy and my family and I lived in Lisbon for a few years, we spent every summer on the Praia do Sul in Ericeira. I know this town.

Moments after our driver drops us on Ericeira's main square, David and I disappear into Ericeira's Old Town. We stroll on old cobble-stoned streets, past white-washed buildings and Mykonos-blue awnings that ooze oceanic charm.

I could live here, David says, almost instantly. The words fall from his mouth, unprompted, unpremeditated. They have a life of their own. *I could live here. I could live here.* The words keep coming. Like David is completely out of control.

When you know you know.

I learn, in this moment, that David is ready to live in a small town. I am ready to live in a small town, as well. Why wait?

It happens fast. February 2024. I travel to Setubal, a larger version of Ericeira, 40 minutes south of Lisbon. I know while I am there. Yes, Setubal. Get myself a Portuguese tax ID. Get myself a Portuguese bank. Get a real estate agent in Setubal. Start looking at neighborhoods, condos. Meet with an accountant in Setubal. Meet with an immigration attorney in Lisbon. Return to Florida. Hire a real estate agent to sell one of my Florida condos. Return to Ericeira and Setubal with David, end of March. Look at neighborhoods, condos in Setubal with David and our agent.

We stay in Fonte Nova. I watch David fall in love with Fonte Nova. I love the Santos Nicolau neighborhood. Love Fonte Nova, as well. Fonte Nova it is. I return in May, look at three apartments to rent in Fonte Nova. Two furnished, one unfurnished. The moment I step into the unfurnished one I know it is the one. The light, the light. It surpasses anything I thought we might find. We hire an interior designer.. Look at mood boards. Start ordering furniture. I take occupancy at the start of July. David arrives 2 weeks later. On August 9, I officially declare my residency in the country of Portugal at Setubal's City Hall.

These are the tactics. Yes, a lot. Action by individual action, not terribly difficult. And mostly quite a lot of fun.

This is the beauty of knowing. You move fast. Get it done.

We don't do years of location scouting. Don't check out every potential destination in Portugal. Don't create plus/minus lists. Refuse to comparison-shop. We have found our town, and we know it.

Wall Street Carol set me free. We're in Setubal. For now. This is an apartment we love. For now. We plan to buy an apartment in our city. We will likely sell that apartment again. May move somewhere else, at some point. In Portugal, not in Portugal. Or we may stay.

Who knows.

THEY WILL BE FINE WITHOUT YOU. REALLY.

Our move across countries and continents elicits heartfelt well-wishes from friends. Most feel compelled to tell us what they love about our new home, Portugal, a country that seems to capture the current Zeitgeist. And folks elaborate on their own longings.

I have always wanted to go to Portugal, writes one acquaintance. *I can't wait to visit Portugal. I love everything I know about Portugal. I can see myself retiring there. It has been on my bucket list for a very long time.*

This acquaintance lives in New York. He has a good job, is financially comfortable. Could fly over to Portugal anytime.

He doesn't want to go, Tom Asacker says. *If he wanted to go, he'd go. He likes the fantasy. Most people prefer their fantasy life. They never go.*

Bucket list. That term gets me riled up. I don't ever use it. When I hear of your bucket list, I hear of all the things you desire, or more precisely, the things you tell yourself you desire but are unwilling to pursue, now. Your bucket list is the story of your life deferred. The longer your bucket list, the bigger your fantasy game.

What are you waiting for?

*****

I would love to move to Portugal, my friend Inez tells me when she hears of my move.

Inez, like me, is European. Inez, as I did, resides in the United States but is not an American citizen. Inez, like me, is at her core a European soul.

Inez has lived in Los Angeles for close to 20 years. Used to be in the Hollywood Hills, now resides in a small apartment in the

Valley. Her son Rudy, his family and the grandchildren, Martin and Emil, live not far from her, also in the Valley.

Inez is done with Los Angeles, and Inez is not ready to leave Los Angeles.

If I didn't have my grandchildren here, Inez tells me with a wistful sigh, *I would be gone.*

*****

Claire is a dear Miami friend. Her husband Peter died 8 years ago, after a long, slow decay from Parkinson's. Claire is a vibrant and beautiful woman in her mid-70s. She has found love again, in the company of Mitchell, a retired accountant from South Africa who showed up in Miami 6 years ago. Over the last 4 years, Mitchell and Claire have roamed the world together.

Mitchell is moving to Portugal. Claire is not.

I need to be close to my daughter and my grandchildren, Claire says.

*****

Liz was one of my first friends in Miami, 20 years ago. She called herself a social entrepreneur before that was a thing. Being in Miami allowed Liz to be an easy flight away from the Caribbean NGOs she partnered with. Liz had an eye for design and fixed up a beautiful mid-century house in Surfside. Put in a glorious lap pool that inspired me to do the same in my house in Hollywood.

When grandmotherhood called, Liz sold her house and moved to New Rochelle, a Connecticut suburb of New York City. Purchased a spacious apartment ten minutes from her daughter Ella's house and Ruby, her granddaughter.

I have no regrets, Liz says to me two and a half years later as she recounts selling her New Rochelle digs and moving to Los Angeles. *But I have learned that I cannot live my life for my family. I can visit my family, anytime. But I don't have to dedicate my entire life to them. I am happiest when I am in LA. I always was. I know that now.*

They love me, Liz elaborates. *They very much do. I saw them perhaps a couple of times a month. They just have no need to see me every weekend*

REGRET IS A BITCH

Let us call him R. R is a celebrated personality in the world of "live your best life" evangelists. He has sold over 20 million books world-wide, is a sought-after keynote speaker, has well over a million followers on Instagram. R just turned 60.

In a social media post, not too long ago, R forcefully denounces the notion of retirement. *I want to be 90*, R affirms, *standing on stages and inspiring people all over the world.*

In other words, I want my 90 to look just like my 60.

Comment after comment on his post applauds R's line of thinking. R is articulating our deep-rooted and culturally-conditioned desire to be able to do that which we love, now, for as long as we can.

Forever, really.

I feel a certain sadness as I reflect on R's affirmation. Forget about the retirement word, for a moment. Where is the sense of curiosity about the life we have not yet lived? The sense of wonder? About how life might be different 30 years from now instead of exactly the same? About what else wants to be discovered and investigated?

See, Carol is my evangelist. I have become a 7-year-guy, give or take a few.

Since life is our most precious gift, writes Maya Angelou in *A Letter to My Daughter*[4], *and since it is given to us to live but once, let us so live that we will not regret.*

We will not ever regret curiosity or a sense of wonder, of that I am certain.

Make them your friend. Notice where they wish to take you. And when you know, have the courage to know that you know.

7 is a beautiful number.

---

[4] Maya Angelou, *A Letter to My Daughter* (Random House, 2008)

Annie Gorce

SERENDIPITOUS JOYS

If Annie Gorce contributed to this book, it is to inspire dreams and the courage to live in those who will read these testimonies.

Her motto: *What lies deepest within us never fades; it finds its way, as long as we listen attentively.*

Born in 1954 in a small village in southwest France, in Aveyron, Annie grew up listening to the patrons at her parents' bar share their opinions, while dreaming of becoming a "healer." After an uneventful school life, she followed a new path to Paris to please others.

Married to a man who supported her in all her endeavors and a mother of two sons, Annie seized every opportunity life offered her. Returning to Aveyron, she built her tools through training in the works of Carl Rogers and as a Master Practitioner of Ericksonian Hypnosis, integrating its spiritual approach.

An experienced trainer in communication and personal development for many years, Annie now offers individual coaching sessions and joyfully leads *The Happiness Workshop* she created ten years ago.

The purpose of this workshop is to share and see life differently—to break free from limiting beliefs and realize what lies deepest within us that never fades, while tuning in to the synchronicities life offers each of us.

Her website: www.annie-gorce.fr

Annie Gorce

SERENDIPITOUS JOYS

The natural tendency of every human being to evolve towards what is constructive drives individuals to fulfill their own potential.

– Carl Rogers on *Personal Power: Inner Strength and its Revolutionary Impact*, Delacorte Press, 1977

BUILDING DREAMS

I am pleased to contribute to this work, first and foremost because of my age. I recently celebrated my 70th birthday, which sharpens my awareness of the passing of time. Secondly, my life story impels me to recount the wisdom of life, its beauty, and the opportunities it presents. It is up to us to be attentive and daring enough to seize them.

I was born in a small village in Aveyron, which meant we were far from many cultural offerings. I was often bored and dreamt of a wondrous elsewhere—Paris.

My parents were tradespeople, not wealthy; however, they enabled me to pursue my studies so that I could have a better life, and as we say in our family, so I would toil less than they did.

As a child, I attended public school and received a religious education, which unbeknownst to me set me on a quest for spirituality. In the early grades, I learned poems and loved the music of the words and the rhythm of the sentences. My Thursday ritual, which took hours, unfolded in front of the large mirror in my parents' bedroom. I would practice these verses with dramatic flair, aware that on Friday I would recite them in front of the class with much less pizazz. I was most likely dreaming of becoming an actress one day. I also wondered about the authors—were they all dead? Were there any living poets?

As the dutiful girl I was, I continued my studies, embracing my father's values. He held technical and scientific studies in high regard, paths he had not been able to follow. I could not disappoint him, so I set aside my passion for literature and psychology. But make no mistake, like a little cat that sleeps with one eye open, this longing lay dormant within me.

After obtaining my high school diploma, I enrolled at the university. I attended courses at the Faculty of Chemistry, Biology, and Geology in Toulouse. I loved genetics and geology, but it wasn't enough! I failed my first year (was it intentional?), though I could not be beaten when it came to cinema.

Realizing that general university studies were not for me, my parents then offered me a vocational course and enrolled me in a private school in Paris to become a Medical Laboratory Technician.

I had achieved my first goal; I was going to continue my studies in PARIS.

LANDING ON MY FIRST STAR

I had just turned twenty and was finally settled in the city of my dreams. Failing a second time was, of course, not an option, so I studied fascinating subjects (!), like 'the biochemical characteristics of Enterobacteriaceae.'

That said, I was fulfilled in other ways. I could visit exhibitions, galleries, and museums. Student discounts allowed me to attend the theater, take mime and tap dance classes, and more.

I had two adult friends I cherished greatly. Jacky was a cultured man who would invite me to the theater, while Gérard, a painter, was a humanist. He gave me two books that opened my mind to different perspectives on the world and life: *Man and His Symbols*[5] by Carl Gustav Jung and the first volume of *Les Chemins de la Sagesse*[6] by Arnaud Desjardins.

---

[5] Carl Gustav Jung, *Man and His Symbols*, New York, Dell Publishing, 1964.

[6] Arnaud Desjardins, *Les Chemins de la Sagesse*, vol. 1, Paris, La Table Ronde, 1969.

With my diploma finally in hand, I landed my first job as a laboratory technician at the renowned Saint-Louis Hospital, known for its famous hematologist, Professor Jean Bernard. My supervisor was Professor Georges Flandrin. He probably doesn't remember me, but I have never forgotten his lesson. One day, I asked him a question—I don't remember what it was—but I will never forget his answer: "I don't know." And this was hematology, his area of expertise, the very field in which he had earned his professorship, and he didn't know! And there I was, fresh out of school, thinking I had to know everything. Thank you, Professor! Through those words, I gained freedom, authenticity, and self-confidence.

I am also grateful to have been entrusted with that first job, where I contributed to your research on specific cells and markers of certain diseases. True, I worked in a room in the basement lit by a skylight, but I felt good there, intellectually stimulated.

Besides work, there was the city of Paris to discover. It was on Boulevard Saint-Michel, one evening strolling with friends, that I met the love of my life. We got married and then became parents to our first and adorable son.

With our new family life, our interests evolved, and the call of my native Aveyron, my country haven, grew stronger until we were convinced that it would be paradise. We had plans to restore my great-grandmother's house and grow flowers in our garden.

My husband could work in my parents' business and help it grow, and I would put my skills to good use at the city's hospital laboratory.

What was said was done, and on March 1st, 1982, I put on my new white lab coat. I met my new colleagues and faced the realities of the profession in a multidisciplinary laboratory within a hospital that provided intensive care, surgery, general medicine, maternity, and geriatrics.

Everything seemed promising, yet for me, it was the beginning of hell.

THE DESCENT INTO HELL

Every job has multiple facets and is performed in an atmosphere shaped by the relationships among colleagues. Gone was the electron microscope! I was discovering a job I had never done before. Faced with highly sophisticated machines requiring electronic skills I didn't have, I admired the engineers who had designed them. In front of these robots, which I had to learn to operate, my biology skills were only useful for validating or rejecting the results they produced.

I was terribly bored, to the point that when I performed serum iron assays, I would mentally sing Bourvil's song, the one where, completely drunk, he sings, 'Yes to iron-rich water! No to alcohol!'[7]

---

[7] The author is referring here to Bourvil's humorous song "La Causerie Anti-Alcoolique (L'eau Ferrugineuse)" from 1951.

As for the interactions with my new colleagues, I would call them catastrophic. It could have been different as I was reunited with women I had known in school and others who had come to the day camp where I had been a counselor. With the latter, we reminisced about our favorite song from that time, 'One evening in his cabin, a little black boy played the guitar… Zoum bada zoum…'

It is important for me today to award the Golden Palm to the most remarkable one, the one who never smiled and who would show me spontaneous hostility. One day, when I mentioned a way of working from my previous job, she replied in a tone I can't quite describe: 'Here, we do things differently. You'll adapt.'

At that time, I knew nothing about group dynamics. I experienced, without understanding, what the anxiety of change and fear of losing power can provoke in people. They had worked together for some time, and the roles they had established could be disrupted by the arrival of a newcomer.

Thankfully, there was Annie, who was kind, and Sylvie, with whom I still share a beautiful friendship today.

EMBRACING CHANGE AS A MATTER OF SURVIVAL

My husband eventually left the family business for a promising career in banking, while I felt myself fading a little more each day. Fortunately, the small spark within me, which had never fully diminished, decided it was time to awaken.

As a young adult, I had neither understood nor dared to give proper place to my aspirations and needs. But now, they could no longer be ignored. It was clear that I was out of place, and to survive, I began attending workshops on morphopsychology and active listening. My husband's support throughout this journey was invaluable. Despite the hundred-kilometer commute, these sessions were a much needed breath of fresh air, and they brought me immense benefits.

It was during these workshops that I discovered the work of Carl Rogers.

A TURNING POINT

Then, as if the stars had truly aligned, I came across an ad in a magazine: "Training in Client-Centered Psychotherapy and Applications of the Person-Centered Approach." Accredited by the American Psychological Association and conducted by the Institut de Lugano in Switzerland—the only institute in Europe founded by Carl Rogers and his colleagues—this training spanned three years, totaling 1,000 hours, divided into short three-day and long ten-day modules.

When it came to financing, the solution appeared. A resourceful friend informed me about training leave offered in hospitals, available exclusively to those pursuing a career change, which fit my situation perfectly. Since psychology was unrelated to medical laboratory analysis, my request was approved. The first session was organized by the Institut de Lugano, after which participants were responsible for arranging the long modules themselves. Facilitators—what others might call trainers—came from the U.S., France, and various European countries. Those who had worked closely with Carl Rogers had a particular aura, in my eyes. This diversity enriched our meetings, and as Rogers stated, "Experience is the supreme authority," and we lived through many.

This path led me to Hungary, Alsace, Brittany, and Savoie—far from the environment I once despised. Carl Jung was right; synchronicity is real. Life placed the right opportunities and people on my path at the right time. I'm truly grateful!

A LIFE TRANSFORMED

My professional and personal life can be divided into two phases, with this training program marking the turning point. Rogers was not just a psychologist; he was a philosopher and humanist. His work centered on a deep trust in human nature, a conviction I had long carried without fully realizing it. Discovering myself in his teachings brought both astonishment and the freedom to truly be myself.

Finally, I was living: Beyond facades,
Beyond 'I shoulds,'
Beyond expectations,
Beyond the duty to please others,
Towards self-direction,

Towards mobility and process,

Towards complexity,

Towards openness to experiences,

Towards acceptance of others,

Towards self-confidence.

NEW ACHIEVEMENTS

Tired of rural life, my husband and I moved to Rodez, a city offering far more professional and cultural opportunities. A friend had recently earned her holistic health counseling certificate, and together, we founded an association called Communication, Aide, Formation, Écoute Humaniste[8] (CAFEH). This legal structure, which I still operate today, allowed us to offer training and support.

For financial reasons, I divided my time between my original profession and this new pursuit. Thanks to various training courses, developments, and opportunities on the side, my role at the lab evolved to a point where I actually enjoyed it. I didn't need to push anyone down the stairs! With the passage of time, old colleagues departed and new, more delightful ones took their place.

However, my fulfillment and creativity could only truly flourish elsewhere, so I eventually left the lab. On my last day, I hosted

---

[8] In English: "Compassionate Communication, Training, and Humanistic Listening Skills"

a farewell party, which, beyond tradition, symbolized the camaraderie we had finally built.

I opened my own practice, where I applied Rogers's approach, guiding clients through personal development. One evening, almost by surprise, I discovered the magnetic energy in my hands. After completing two Reiki modules and attuning to what I call my guides—the intelligence that surrounds and inspires us when we pay attention to it—I developed my own energy technique, which I use for addressing physical ailments and energetic rebalancing.

A CAREER AS A TRAINER

Becoming a trainer in communication and personal development was another goal of mine, and so I submitted my resume to the head of this sector at the Chamber of Commerce and Industry (CCI). Unfortunately, there were no openings at the time.

But life has a sense of humor. Shortly thereafter, that very person called me in distress—a trainer had canceled, leaving a group of trainees without an instructor. "If you are able to step up to the challenge, I won't forget it," he told me. And I did, and he kept his word. For the next thirty years, I taught at the CCI, for both adults in companies and young people completing their studies. Words cannot express the joy I experienced during that time. It was a period full of rich exchanges—creating modules, developing educational tools, inventing exercises—and my passion for creativity was fulfilled.

My guiding principle remained the same: to foster self-confidence in participants, stimulate their creativity, encourage their authenticity, and provide communication tools. The evaluations of my modules confirmed my success: "A trainer who listens and is kind and knows how to bring our qualities to the forefront. She encourages us to change our perspective on ourselves and our interpersonal relationships. She is passionate and dynamic."

NEW ENCOUNTERS, NEW DISCOVERIES, NEW TOOLS

Thanks to a friend, I discovered Conversation Papillon, a training website offering online conferences led by experts in spirituality, health, and well-being.

A significant turning point came when I met Isabelle David, founder of ID Com International in Canada. I completed programs in aura reading and Ericksonian and conversational hypnosis, eventually becoming certified as a Master Practitioner. Thanks to technology and the possibilities of video conferencing, I could train remotely. However, during a visit to our son in Montreal, I took advantage of the opportunity to attend an in-person module—it was indeed better that way!

Isabelle is an extraordinary woman who guides others spiritually and technically through teachings in hypnosis, NLP, and coaching. Her training course, infused with compassion, helps everyone discover their true selves. My encounter with Isabelle inspired a new evolution in my practice. I began integrating conversational hypnosis into my communication modules and offered Ericksonian hypnosis sessions for individual clients.

A SOURCE OF PRIDE: L'ATELIER BONHEUR

For over a decade, I've been leading "L'Atelier Bonheur" ("The Happiness Workshop") at Rodez Cultural Center. The program, inspired by Carl Rogers's group work, aims to foster discussion, challenge limiting beliefs to make room for empowering ones, explore concepts like Carl Jung's "happy coincidences," build self-confidence, and delve into spirituality and philosophy.

As a facilitator, I see this as another way to guide each person towards themselves. The diversity, richness, and inner beauty of human nature continue to amaze me.

BEING ELECTED TO A MUNICIPAL OFFICE

Another twist of fate! One evening, I went to a dinner hosted by a friend who was politically active. Due to the gender balance requirements, his group needed more women to complete the list of candidates they were presenting for the municipal elections. I agreed but made sure to specify my conditions: "Yes, but put me at the bottom of the list." That was meant to ensure I would be elected without having to actively engage in municipal affairs. Yet, the unfolding events led me to take on the roles of Deputy Mayor and Vice-President of the Consortium of Cities in charge of the Local Security and Delinquency Prevention Council (CLSPD in French).

Through these positions, I discovered the world of politics and the impact that local elected officials can have on their communities. It was a profound learning experience for me. I had the opportunity to meet remarkable individuals and confront realities I had never encountered before, such as violence against women. Those seven years of discoveries and valuable lessons left a lasting impression on my life and philosophy.

EPILOGUE

This journey, briefly recounted here, and the experiences that have shaped it attest to what for me was long a belief and has since become a certainty: *Nothing is impossible!* If I had remained comfortably ensconced in my Parisian laboratory, what would my life have become? Would I have even had the chance to discover my true self?

All the insights gained during these training courses would have remained unknown, and I would have missed out on meeting all the wonderful souls who awakened me, all of whom I haven't mentioned by name.

Yes, life is a turbulent and sometimes violent ocean, but it opens the way to beautiful coincidences. We find ourselves unexpectedly docking at the most magnificent of harbors.

To all of you reading these stories, I hope I have encouraged you to embrace your own *"Audacity to Live."*

Crystal Weber

LEARNING TO BE ME

A writer at heart, Crystal Weber works as a translator and interpreter from French and Spanish into English. She was born in California and currently lives in France. She has always been passionate about dance and more recently yoga. She finds her inspiration in the glimmers of her daily experience.

Crystal fell ill with breast cancer in 2018 and has now been in remission for four years. Her experience with illness pushed her on a quest to get to know her real self and to heal. For this, yoga has been an essential tool. In 2020, she completed a yoga teacher training programme and has been teaching hatha flow yoga classes on the side for two years.

Currently, she is enrolled in a yoga therapy course and in the future aims to offer one-on-one consultations to help people heal and find peace in their lives regardless of what ails them. She would also like to focus on supporting cancer patients during and after their treatments through yoga therapy.

To find out more about Crystal,
visit: www.crystalnicoleweber.com

Crystal Weber

LEARNING TO BE ME

We must stop being who we think we are and become

who we truly are.

– Unknown

The trees. They were the ones who instigated it. They were the ones who chanted in my ears, "Do it, don't hold back. Do it, don't hold back." I was sitting on the ground, at the base of a Sequoia in the middle of the Bois de Boulogne in Paris, tears streaming down my cheeks. My forehead was burning hot from a fever that would not subside, and my eyesight was blurry. I had been sick in bed for days with some strange ailment. It was not the coronavirus, it was not the flu. The doctors blamed it on a virus, but it was the second time this strange virus had struck in the span of 2 months, pinning me to my bed for weeks on end. Despite my weakness, I needed to get out. I needed to see the trees.

There in the middle of the woods, with the clarity of nature, a door opened and I could finally feel the anger boiling under my skin. It was wreaking havoc on my insides, had been for several years. "Do it, don't hold back. Do it, don't hold back," they chanted louder and louder all around me. The material form of the trees started to dissipate into the air, leaving behind only their rainbow essence. Towers of light shot out from the ground in every which direction. "Do it, don't hold back. Do it, don't hold back," they egged me on.

And then... I snapped or rather let go. An unexpected scream. "AHHHHHHHHHHHHHHHHHHHHHHHHHHHHHH!" – bellowed from somewhere deep inside me and resonated throughout the Bois de Boulogne. Years of energetic accumulation of frustration and injustice were released into the universe. Once the sound subsided, my first reflex was to look around and see if anyone had heard or seen me. There was nobody. Just the trees, back in their physical form, and they were all laughing and applauding me. I couldn't help but let a smile spread across my face.

That was when I decided enough was enough. The next day I quit my job.

REFLECTIONS ON LIGHT

I had been working in an unhealthy office environment for over two years as a translator and interpreter. There was no room for creativity, no room for questions, no room for women. Men ruled.

Respect for hierarchy and obedience were the main values. Rules were strict, yet conveniently bent to serve the interests of those in power. That word still makes me shiver. *Power.* How many times did I hear, "I am the one in power. You must simply do what you are told"… The way things worked at the office was absurd. There were no processes, no direction, no support, no accountability from our superiors. Everything was always the fault of the "bottom-feeders." Emotional intelligence and employee well-being were not even on the radar. I felt like I was on a ship being sailed into rough waters by a band of bottle-loving pirates, whose outlandish egos were deemed sufficient to compensate for their lack of nautical knowledge. But we all know that an over dimensioned ego is bound to sink. Even though I was hired to scrub the decks, they had silently placed the responsibility of ensuring the survival of the mission on my shoulders. A one-way ticket to walk the plank.

I felt mistreated, undervalued, powerless and above all doomed, but it was easy to convince myself to stay for the sake of financial security. I would set artificial deadlines to make my days more digestible, "Just 6 more months, just 3 more months, just 1 more month..." At first, I tried to fight and stand up for what was right, but I soon realized that my efforts were pointless. 'Power' always won, no matter how absurd the battle. That was when I closed my eyes and let the ship take its chaotic course. Apathy slowly took over and everything became sapped of meaning.

Then the dreams started...

Where has the light gone?

It was the middle of the night and I was in my office, sitting behind my computer in the dark. My body was weighed down by fatigue and I felt drained of all energy. I rested my head on my desk, too exhausted to work. A light emanated from my colleague's office opposite mine illuminating a triangular patch of the darkened corridor. I could hear my boss inside yelling my name, "Crystal!? Where's Crystal?! She has no light in her office! Where has the light gone?" I lifted my head and switched on the small desk lamp next to my computer but it immediately flickered off. My head fell back down on my desk, exhausted from the effort. The shouting continued. "Crystal!? Crystal!? Where has the light gone?" I did not have the energy to reply, so I lay there, motionless, with my head resting on my desk seeking respite in what was my new darkened state of lethargic apathy.

The power of light

Again, it was the middle of the night. This time I was in my apartment, plunged in darkness, and a heavy, dark presence had been chasing me throughout the different rooms. I couldn't see it but I could sense it. At first, I was scared, and tried to run away but my attempts at escape were futile against a force that was omnipresent. Every time I tried to switch the lights on, "it" turned them off, plunging me into ultimate darkness. It seemed to be reveling in my frenzied disarray. Finally aware of the triviality of my flight efforts against its evil game, I stopped running. In the kitchen I decided to face it. I stood firmly with my two feet rooted in the ground as an enormous surge of anger pulsated through my body. When it was too much to contain, I let it explode into a scream that reached the heavens 'I hate you!!!!!!!!!!!!!!!!!! Fuck you!!!!!!!!!!!!!!!!!!!!!!!!!!!!!!' (Pardon my French).

The anger dissolved my physical body into a powerful current of energy and light that shook the ground and blasted through the ceiling of my apartment and upwards towards the night sky. The power of it all was so intense, it took me by surprise. This power, my power, scared me. I stood in my kitchen for a few seconds waiting to be consumed by the force of my anger, but rather than drain me it made me stronger. And that's when the lights in my apartment came back on... and stayed on for good.

The message was clear. I had lost my light in this unhealthy office environment but I had not lost my determination to get it back.

People around me warned me not to quit. They advised me to go on sick leave, to go to court for moral harassment, and all sorts of other solutions that would have dragged out my time there, but I did not listen to them.

First lesson: I learned to trust my own inner compass rather than relying on that of others.

I listened to my body. It was manifesting the suffering that I had kept inside—in the form of strange rashes and fevers—and

I had already been down that road and didn't want to repeat. No, I was not going to have unemployment benefits and no, I did not have a job lined up. I had nothing, just a strong desire to be free to live the life I really wanted, the life I deserved, but that was enough.

REFLECTIONS ON FREEDOM

It was soon clear that freedom was going to be much more than just freedom from my office job. It was also going to have to be freedom from myself. The first step in building my new life was to figure out what I wanted to do. When I have deep existential questions, I often consult my library. So, one afternoon, I plopped myself on the floor in front of my bookcase, cleared my mind, and asked the universe, "What life is the best life for me to build?" I randomly reached for a book on the shelves and opened it to a page at whim. To my surprise, the page was completely blank. I chuckled and understood that I needed to do the work but that everything was possible. I am the author of the story of my life, and there is no better place to start than with a blank page.

So, I let myself dream up the wildest lives: travel for 6 months through Sri Lanka, India, and Costa Rica on a spiritual quest; move back to California, become a writer, and live in a small wooden cabin by the sea; set up a yoga studio and healing practice in the south of France; become a dancer and choreographer in Paris. Soon after, my ideas were met with a cascade of limiting thoughts: "I don't have the money to travel for 6 months, I'm not good enough to become a writer, there are already so many yoga studios, I'm too old to become a dancer". Then, I remembered the blank page. I remembered my power in my dream. I remembered the trees, "Do it, don't hold back."

Second lesson: I allowed everything to be possible.

All of these lives were possible if I really wanted them. I just had to align my heart, body and mind and embark down a path. So, I asked these parts of me, "What do you really want right now?" The answer was clear. My heart and body wanted to dance. The excitement of my childhood dream of becoming a dancer came rushing back to me, sending ripples of joy throughout my body. Ok, let's dance.

So, during my first months of unemployment, I did just that. I danced. I took classes, workshops, discovered new styles, allowed myself to take the advanced classes I thought I was not good enough for. I set my limiting thoughts aside and did what I loved. No, I was not making money (yet) but I was nourishing my body and soul.

This soul food was fertilizer for other ideas to flourish. Eventually something began to materialize from within, and I was able to understand the connections between my different interests and passions. From all the different areas I dabbled in—yoga, yoga therapy, dance, art, reiki, writing, feng shui—it became clear that I wanted to choreograph and use movement and energy to heal. The details were far from being clear but the concept had finally sprouted.

As for the limiting thoughts, it was and still is not easy to put them aside because they always come back and sometimes at full force. With them, they bring fear. In my case, it was mainly the fear of not having enough money to pay for my mortgage, bills, and food (and still is to be honest). After months of not having a revenue, the fear was real and it was telling me to get another office job and abandon my ridiculous dreams. And I listened for a while, focusing my energy on finding a "proper" job, but I was met with nothing but closed doors. Rejection after rejection for positions I was more than qualified for, but also positions I did not really want.

I realized then that my actions were not aligning with my real desires. I decided to give myself the benefit of the doubt, to use those limiting thoughts to learn more about who I was and as fuel to allow myself to grow to my full potential. I felt that there was a lot of untapped energy in me that could make really beautiful things happen if given the chance.

Third lesson: I vowed to no longer make decisions from a place of fear, but rather a place of love.

A love for myself, and love for my potential. I am not meant to live in a cage or scrub the decks. It's my time to shine. When I put fear to rest and decided to believe in myself, that's when mysterious things started to happen.

REFLECTIONS ON SYNCHRONICITIES

I recently moved to a new neighborhood and near my house there is a cultural center that offers a rich program of activities. Every day I would walk past it and say to myself, "I need to go in there and check it out." This train of thought went on for a good two months until finally one day, in mid-June, I woke up thinking "Today is the day. I must go to that cultural center TODAY." The urge was too strong to fight and so I went, not really knowing what the purpose of my visit was.

Once I was there, I decided I would ask them if I could rent a rehearsal room. I had been longing for a space to just dance and create. The secretary distractedly responded to my queries as she shuffled papers on her desk. Without looking at me, she asked, "What kind of activity do you want to rehearse?" as if just going through the motions.

"I want a space where I can dance," I replied.

She paused, lifted her nose out of her papers, and looked me in the eyes with curiosity, "What kind of dance?" she inquired.

"Contemporary," I said without hesitation.

Her eyes lit up and her facial features softened. "It just so happens we are desperately looking for a contemporary dance teacher. Would you be interested? If so, I can introduce you to the director right away."

Obviously, I accepted and within seconds was sitting in front of the director explaining my dance experience. He seemed genuinely interested and scheduled an official interview in two days' time. I skipped out of the cultural center floating on clouds. I could not believe my luck!

However, the laws of the material world still apply. Dreams do not come true in a snap of the fingers.

Fourth lesson: Sometimes I must let go of what I want to make room for what is really supposed to happen.

I went to my interview at the cultural center confidently thinking that the job was mine. Instead, the director announced to me that unfortunately he could not hire me because I do not have the famous French Diplôme d'État in dance. He also announced that he could not hire me as a yoga teacher either because the center already had one and that would create unwanted competition. "Great, dead end!" I thought to myself.

"But..." he continued. "If you're interested, the center can finance your diploma in dance. In the meantime, we have a free spot on Tuesday evenings from 7 to 9:30pm. What classes can you offer?"

With renewed hope, I pitched my ideas for movement classes based on yoga, intuitive dance, and dance therapy and he was in! He loved the ideas and added my classes to the schedule right then and there.

Fifth lesson: Always give priority to my intuition and act in accordance with it, no matter how outrageous its 'urges' may seem.

It wasn't long before the next 'urge' struck. One morning, I was impelled to visit a center for associations, also located in my neighborhood. I went thinking that I would leave flyers for my summer yoga lessons in the park. The lady at the counter was stiff and her features were closed off when I asked her if I could leave flyers.

"Are you an association?" she asked with an accusatory tone.

"No. I am a freelancer," I replied with a tinge of shame.

"Then no, you may absolutely not leave flyers here. This is a place for associations, and you are not an association so we cannot help you," she lectured me.

Again, the rules of the material world apply. I was taken aback but for some reason I persisted.

"You see I have this idea...." and I ensued to explain to her my idea around yoga and movement.

She listened attentively and ended up scribbling an email on a piece of paper and handing it to me.

The email was a generic one for the event planning department at the Town Hall. I thanked her and left a bit discouraged. That afternoon I wrote the email pitching my idea, thinking "well this is bound to get lost in the ether of online communication."

The very next day, I received a call from the Director of Health at the Town Hall!

"I've been forwarded your email and I am very interested in your idea. The town is organizing a Semaine de la Santé[9] in a few months' time. I would love to meet you and see how we can collaborate."

The meeting went well, and I walked away with a collaboration with the Town Hall for movement workshops during their Semaine de la Santé. I thanked my lucky stars.

It seemed as if the ball had been set in motion. From there, I received yet another mysterious call:

"Hello, I've seen the workshops you are organizing for the Town Hall, and I would like to meet you to see if we can set up a collaboration for senior citizens."

The meeting went well and I walked away with a collaboration to teach yoga to senior citizens once a month and to participate in the Forum des Seniors. I once again thanked my lucky stars.

Sixth lesson: The people I was meant to work with will find me, they will see me.

More calls and text messages started to come in from people who were looking for yoga classes, coaching sessions, cultural activities, dance workshops... not everything has materialized into work but I feel like I've put the ingredients into the pot and now the pot is simmering, cooking up things far better than I could have ever imagined. Good things take time.

---

[9] *Semaine de la Santé* translates to "Health Week" in English, an event dedicated to promoting health awareness and activities.

Reflections on success

It took me a long time to accept, really accept to participate in this book. I still struggle with legitimacy. Am I really what I say I am? And the hardest part is not convincing others of my worth, but convincing myself of my worth. But I know that once I see my worth, others will see it too.

I still do not make enough money to live from my new activity and I still have a lot of formal education to complete. But I realized that success is not about money or education. Success is about tapping into your talent and sharing it with others from a place of authenticity and love for what you do. Success is not about the result, but about having the audacity to try and to put yourself out there.

We live in a results-driven world that places priority on productivity. When we do not produce the desired results, we may be reprimanded by our superiors or ourselves and our confidence takes a hit. In reality, we do not have control over the outputs, only the inputs. This is why I've decided that I am not a human-doing that produces results; I am a human-being. The cry that I let out in the Bois de Boulogne of Paris was a cry to the world and to myself that said, "Basta, let me be who I was meant to be."

And the outcome of all of this? Well, I'll leave that up to the trees.

Isa Lichtenthurn

THE ENDLESS REALM OF POSSIBILITIES

Raised in a family where anything was always possible, I was encouraged from a young age to pursue my dreams.

At 15, as an apprentice in a travel agency, I earned my first paycheck, and three years later, I set off on a backpacking journey through Asia and Australia.

At 28, I left Switzerland once again with my partner for a round-the-world trip. Along the way, in a Mexican hospital, I was diagnosed with lymphoma. I cut the journey short and returned to Switzerland.

In addition to standard allopathic treatment, I discovered gentle therapies that addressed both body and soul. In 2000, I co-founded

L'Intermed with my sister—a space for sharing and guidance in alternative therapies, a kind of Doctissimo ahead of its time.

In 2002, my transformation began. Embracing a spirit of freedom and change, we moved to Provence and renovated an old farmhouse into a guesthouse. Our concept, innovative for the time, centered on well-being: morning yoga, massages, and healthy, delicious meals to delight our guests.

In 2011, our entrepreneurial spirit resurfaced. We sold *Felisa* and embarked on a monumental project: renovating a sanatorium perched on a cliff.

In 2019, we decided to sell and reinvent ourselves elsewhere. We settled in the Algarve, where I immersed myself in artistic creation by opening *Atelier33* and sharing my passion for cooking through volunteer work with a local association.

Facebook: https://www.facebook.com/atelier33algarve

Isa Lichtenthurn

THE ENDLESS REALM OF POSSIBILITIES

Everyone thinks of changing the world, but no one thinks of changing themselves.

– Leo Tolstoy

Today, with connected glasses, we can experience virtual reality and travel to "extraordinary" places. The sun always shines, the sea is a turquoise blue, and a perfect breeze blows. But is this really traveling?

For me, traveling means losing oneself a little to better find oneself; it has always held a predominant place in my life. What I love most about traveling is not having a schedule, waking up with the sun, going to bed when I'm tired, and forgetting the time, crying in front of a breathtaking landscape, walking barefoot in the mud at low tide, tasting a traditional dish, discovering new flavors, visiting the local market, settling down in a place, and putting down temporary roots. I delight in beauty and nature, unafraid of rainy days, joyfully accepting everything as it is. I avoid the guidebook's "must-see" spots and instead prefer to try something new each day, with a childlike sense of wonder, no expectations, and a heart full of awe.

In 1999, after five months in Quito, Ecuador, my partner and I savored the freedom of travel, setting out with the goal of circling the globe. We crossed multiple borders on foot, climbed the 1,200 stone steps of the Lost City on trembling legs after battling a stubborn bout of food poisoning, slept under the stars in hammocks surrounded by mosquitoes, and tended to blisters after countless days of hiking. We even played adventurers, discovering an atoll of paradisiacal islands off the coast of Panama, diving into turquoise waters surrounded by a kaleidoscope of colors. Such wonderful memories!

The wound is the place where the light enters you.

– Rumi

As our journey progressed, my body began to transform in alarming ways. We decided to clarify the situation by making an appointment at the American Hospital in Mexico City.

Clicerio, an empathetic and deeply kind oncologist—who would later play the role of matchmaker by organizing an unforgettable love-filled wedding celebration for us—delivered the news: advanced-stage lymphoma cancer. The rest of the story became more grounded in reality. We returned to Switzerland to continue living.

Chemotherapy began, bringing with it a series of physical and emotional trials. My hair fell out in handfuls, my belly swelled, I couldn't stop vomiting, and my energy evaporated. I became dependent on others for even the simplest tasks. Thankfully, my loved ones surrounded me with unconditional love and support. "You have to fight!" they told me. Fight against myself? But I wasn't at war with my body.

So, I decided to embrace life as it was, with its ups and downs. I took charge, realizing that, in the end, I was the only one responsible for my health and the person I wanted to become. Day by day, I began to feel more aligned. I started to see cancer not as an enemy but as a messenger. It pushed me to reevaluate my priorities. I began meditating, changed my diet, learned to eat healthily, and listened to my body. Each day became an opportunity to say a big "yes" to everything that is and to express gratitude for every little thing.

For two years, I experienced illness. I emerged from it stronger, more serene, and ready to embrace whatever the future held with a smile and an open heart. When I think of my journey around the world, I realize it took an unexpected turn: I traveled within myself, and I feel profoundly grateful.

During the chemotherapy sessions, I encountered many people grappling with loneliness and confusion, blindly following the dogmatic advice of their doctors, unaware that other approaches could complement conventional treatments. As for me, I was fortunate. Philippe, my partner and life companion, had long ago opened the door to "other possibilities." Thanks to him, I explored various natural therapies alongside allopathic treatments.

I fasted, underwent the Ayurvedic Panchakarma cure—a detoxification and purification process—and met fascinating individuals. My thirst for learning even took me to Quebec, where I ultimately discovered that everything I needed was already within me. I received so many massages that I must have been ready to be served on a platter!

Art therapy, Feldenkrais method, naturopathy, reflexology, sophrology, family constellations—soon none of these held any secrets from me. This treasure trove of knowledge accumulated during my illness spoke to me... Why not share it?

SHARING EXPERTISE AND FOLLOWING THE FLOW OF DREAMS

Together with my sister Laetitia, we founded *L'Intermed*, a space dedicated to listening, exchange, and personal development. Our mission was simple: to offer everyone the chance to change perspectives, explore new horizons, and provide a genuine springboard toward a brighter future.

Depending on each person's needs, we introduced various physical and psychological therapies without providing a formal diagnosis. Each client left with suggestions for therapies to explore, the contact details of specialists, and perhaps the sense of having broadened their horizons.

What followed was a rich period of sharing, focused on others, with kindness and respect. Looking back, I realize I've always loved the excitement of new projects. Those creative and slightly naive firsts have always uplifted me and given me wings. Even today, I love making pros-and-cons lists, sketching out a future kitchen, drafting business plans, switching hats to play the architect, the builder, or the chef.

Our past, fears, and conditioning create our limits. Freeing ourselves from them without fear or prejudice is one of life's most precious gifts. Philippe and I had a dream: to move to the south of France, bask in the sun, rely on no one but ourselves, and create a different kind of living space centered on well-being, joy, and simplicity.

In 2002, driven by our desire for change, we made our dream a reality. We left Switzerland and settled in a small village in the Gard region. What followed was a period of intense learning—everything was new. So many magnificent firsts!

I still remember the satisfaction I felt after building my first wall! When we installed the concrete sink we had created from scratch in the garden, I was elated! The miles of lime plaster, the tendonitis in my right wrist from overusing a jackhammer, all left their mark on my body.

A construction site is a perfect metaphor for life—it's a bit like a rollercoaster, taking you from moments of intense joy to deep despair.

I had countless doubts during the work: Would the rooms be soundproof enough? How would we manage parking in the garden? Would we have enough money to finish? Should we keep the metal beam running through the kitchen? Would we finish on time? Why wasn't the plumber here today? How could we renovate the roof without breaking the bank? Sleepless nights of overthinking, exhausting days with gloves in the cement mixer and a trowel in hand, building the garden shed walls… and so many other challenges.

Yet not for one moment did I doubt the success of our project, and the rest of the story proved me right.

They did not know it was impossible, so they did it.

– Mark Twain

We are our own limits, and turning dreams into reality is a gift I've given myself many times.

Our guesthouse, *Felisa*, dressed itself in its finest attire. We traded our work overalls for shorts and sandals, and everything was ready! Still, we were a little nervous about learning a new trade on the job. Sharing a meal, joyful moments, laughter, a good book, or philosophical discussions is one thing—but running a house is a whole different challenge! Would we love it?

I adored every moment. What a privilege it was to practice such a beautiful profession for 20 years.

We kicked off our first season at full speed. Thanks to the early days of the internet, the house was full. We had envisioned a concept around well-being, returning to my first passions: a weeklong package with morning yoga, massages, and dinner every evening.

By the end of December that first year, we were happy but exhausted. It was clear we needed to reevaluate our priorities. Being your own boss has one wonderful advantage—you can set your life's clock however you like.

What wonderful encounters! Very often, when the door opened to welcome new guests, I felt as though I recognized them, which brought a delightful ease to our relationships. I wanted to pamper them, anticipate their needs, and delight them. I prepared bowls of milk infused with essential oils, wonderfully fragrant, to add to their jacuzzi baths, helping to relax sore muscles or soothe sensitive souls.

I discovered myself to be a cook and was captivated by the marvelous alchemy of cooking for others. It felt as though I already knew how to cook. I didn't seek inspiration from books but instead ventured into creating new recipes. What thrilled me the most were those moments between my creative thoughts and the dish I was about to serve. At some point, everything simply fell into place. To my absolute delight, I realized I had a small gift: I only needed to think about a combination of ingredients, and I could already taste it in my mind. From that moment, I had endless fun, especially with savory dishes. As for the rigor required in desserts—with their precise measurements and waiting times—this was one of the reasons I eventually turned to acrylic painting, but I digress!

Because our guests had no expectations, I felt no pressure. I was free. I remember some epic evenings, like the one where, following a power outage, I had to quickly change the menu by headlamp because the rosemary veal roast, slowly cooking in the oven, would never be done in time! Or the wild night when we had to serve our guests with smiles on our faces while outside, a deluge threatened to flood us at any moment.

We found a rhythm that suited us perfectly: seven months of intense work, one month for small renovations, and, best of all, four months of travel.

It was during this time that we made the choice to remain just the two of us and not expand our family. We didn't feel the need to leave a legacy, and deep down, I had the intimate conviction that I had already given, perhaps in other lives!

BEING THE CREATOR OF ONE'S OWN LIFE IS SUCH A BEAUTIFUL CRAFT.

In 2009, a burst of madness overtook us, and we embarked on a new adventure. The challenge: renovating a 19th-century four-story building perched above a gorge—a massive undertaking! A year of intense work followed, with endless days, aching bodies, and doubts. Yet we always had the desire to surpass ourselves and the feeling that anything was possible, that everything naturally fell into place when our hearts were aligned—the joyful theater of life.

And so, the carousel spun again. Our new guesthouse *Metafort* opened its doors and brought us eight years of immense happiness. I thank you from the bottom of my heart, wonderful guests; because of you, those years were fantastic.

I've never been materially attached to the places I've lived, but that house—perched atop a village like something out of a fairytale—touched me deeply.

Sitting on the wall overlooking the gorge, my feet dangling over the edge, I felt connected to something greater, and it was magical.

Freedom was what I loved most about this profession. But, as in life, everything changes. New rules emerged—no more trusty paper agenda, and hello large online booking platforms. Before bitterness set in, we decided to sell and, once again, step out of our comfort zone. We left France and placed the belongings of a lifetime in a container headed for the the Algarve, southern Portugal.

What amazes me about these transitions is having a partner who feels the same things I do, who shares the same desires at the same time. It brings a wonderful lightness and dynamic energy.

For this new adventure, we envisioned ourselves as builders, ecological entrepreneurs, and permaculture farmers—all at once. It sounded perfect!

Our plan was clear: to build self-sufficient homes using raw earth. To this end, we imagined various systems to conserve water, from greywater recovery to patios designed to avoid the need for air conditioning. We spent days drawing up plans, researching innovative ecological building materials, and, to top it off, we bought two plots of land.

Writing this makes me laugh out loud because what followed was entirely different—thanks to Covid. In Portugal, too, this was a time of standstill, so we took the time to live, explore the region, and talk with local builders. We met many people like us, expats from all over the world, and we came to understand that everything here was different: the rules, the way people work, the paperwork, the bureaucracy, and so on.

We arrived with oversized egos, in full 'I-know-it-all' mode, but we quickly had to rethink our approach! After making our famous pros-and-cons list, everything became clear. We were going to live, not do!

I am a big fan of those moments when, in clarity and surrender, everything falls into place—you just have to ask. A bit simplistic, I admit, but when I look back, I see that my whole life has unfolded this way. Coincidences, destiny?

Here, in the charming town of Olhão, I find myself once again. Living by the sea wasn't on my wish list. Thankfully, I didn't give it much thought, or I would have missed out on this incredible experience. Within a ten-minute walk, I reach the lagoon, an expanse of blue as far as the eye can see—except at low tide. Every six hours, the water empties like a bathtub; the landscape completely transforms into a new world.

Across the way, paradisiacal islands of white sand with dreamy names—Armona, Deserta, Culatra—have been our playground for four years.

Let the beauty of what you love be what you do.

– Rumi

When I started painting 20 years ago, it was to decorate the walls of *Felisa*. Later, I created a small 5-square-meter studio overlooking the gorges, where I could paint both indoors and outdoors at *Metafort*. I played the artist's role, and I liked it. In fact, when

I donned my painter's smock, I sometimes sold a painting, still wet, to a guest.

In this stage of my life, I see things on a larger scale. With a Belgian artist friend, we opened *Atelier 33*. The goal isn't to take ourselves too seriously but to explore, with joy and good humor. I love trying different approaches, stepping outside the box, and using unique materials. Currently, I'm experimenting with burlap and loving it. I play with textures, add plaster, chalk, ashes from my fireplace, even stitch two canvases together. A delightful, chaotic mess!

The studio is a space for free creation, without schedules. In today's world, where everything is structured, organized, and planned, we delight in being disruptors. If there's one thing I've learned, it's that life is short, and there's no right or wrong—there's this beautiful song that resonates within each of us, whispering that everything IS perfect, nothing to do, nothing to change.

Living in this beautiful country of Portugal fulfills me. I didn't want to be here in Olhão as a mere observer but to take part in the local life. So I learned Portuguese and wanted to give back to my new community.

I met an angel, Patricia, who, during Covid, created the Love for All association to help the underprivileged. For the past two years, every Friday, when available, I've cooked for 40 human souls in need. I've found a new family—caring, joyful. I belong here, and it's just perfect!

In this love story with Portugal, we visited the Azores and fell in love with the island of Pico. Here, in the middle of the Atlantic, on this volcanic rock that reminds me of the origins of the Earth, I feel perfectly aligned, certain that I'm in the right place. I experience my deepest self and feel connected to everything, linked from the depths of the Earth to the stars. A divine introspection fills me with gratitude. I am in awe of the beauty, of this pure, untamed nature that doesn't need us, where each day dawns for an eternal beginning. And what if Atlantis really existed!

I can't end this chapter without mentioning my beloved. As I write these lines, we're celebrating 25 years of marriage—a quarter-century of intense happiness!

I love traveling by your side, waking up every morning next to you, your calmness, your patience, your persistence when faced with challenges, your vision of the universe, your openness to spiritual dimensions, your handyman skills, and all the little things that make you the wonderful man I journey with.

Throughout our travels, there have been a few storms and squalls, but knowing we were always there for each other, no matter what life had in store, is the greatest gift. Philippe, you are my sailor with a big heart, my compass, and I thank the universe for bringing you into my life.

This universe is not outside of you. Look inside yourself;
everything you want, you already are.

– Rumi

Florence Bibollet

MY FREEDOM

Born in 1967, I discovered yoga at the age of 35.

Sitting on my mat, I immediately felt the undeniable pull of remaining still in silence. For me, it was a radical and, in some ways, sacred act. This marked the beginning of a long journey to learn about myself.

I quickly began my first Viniyoga training in 2004 and started offering group classes for everyone by 2007. Later, I earned a diploma from the Yoga Therapy Institute and trained in Vinyasa and Yin Yoga. I now also organize individual sessions and various workshops.

My role is simply to help people welcome themselves as they are, prioritizing gentleness and rest—luxuries in our busy times.

In parallel, I teach French to foreigners, which enriches me with exposure to other cultures.

Continuously seeking to better define what health truly means, I take a close interest in the benefits of integrative medicine. I am active in an association that supports cancer patients, focusing on the metabolic approach to this condition.

Email: bibolletflorence@gmail.com
Facebook: Alpesyogatherapie

Florence Bibollet

MY FREEDOM

Light can only come from embracing darkness.

– Annick de Souzenelle

1. Flight

As far back as I can remember, my mother had always re-proached me for being different, as if being unique were both a defect and a threat.

I was the quietest, most obedient child, yet I cultivated this difference into a silent and unsuspected disobedience. Seeking to escape the constraints of family life, unable to define my place within it, I found refuge in dreams. Feeding the "No" within, I cut myself off from reality, learning to become elusive, beyond reach. I hid to build my world; it was a possible path to my freedom.

For so long, this small voice urged me to flee the groups that welcomed me as a member, the men who loved me too much, the conversations where everyone agrees. How boring!

Not being where I am expected gives me a certain pleasure laced with arrogance, where I seek to create contradiction. For me, life is movement; consensus is stifling. Single-mindedness drives me mad.

Throughout my life, I realized that behind this fierce and prideful reaction to avoid confinement lay a fear of abandonment. In response to the control exerted over me since childhood, combined with my mother's emotional instability, I was immersed in an insecure environment, lacking a comforting structure, constantly fearing her bouts of fury that threw me into a terrifying no-man's land. At times, I used provocation just to catch my breath.

In choosing the path of yoga, which I interpreted as a journey toward freedom, I felt the need to contradict my fellow teachers. I criticized their need to belong to a community and what I perceived as an ideological and sectarian drift within them. Never enter yoga as one enters a religion.

In our societies, the role of a yoga teacher is often idealized. Yet I was far from embodying the fantasy of the ever-zen teacher with impeccable lifestyle habits. Partly out of defiance, and mostly because I didn't feel up to the spiritual path, I struggled to fully commit. My approach, though sincere, was still tentative. I sometimes felt out of step with others.

I have the impression that we spend most of our time running away from ourselves. When I separated from the father of my children, I blocked the emotional currents surging within me, trying to act courageous, obeying the command to "be strong!" In doing so, I buried a deep sadness and refused to give in to the anger simmering inside; this had a disastrous effect on my health.

What message do we send our children when we deny our negative emotions? We teach them that their feelings cannot be validated. I convinced myself that what I was going through wasn't that serious; inside, it was chaos. My body absorbed the shock, and then I chose to ignore its warning signs.

2. Our Power is Immense

Yes, I deeply believed in spiritual commitment—but I believed in it for others, not for myself! Then, little by little, as I learned to love myself, I realized that I had been idealizing others' potential while neglecting my own. If I could believe in others' strength, why not believe in mine as well? What are our heroes if not a projection of our idealized selves?

Today, I see that a renowned artist, a distinguished scientist, the first man to set foot on the moon—figures I once placed in an absolute, unattainable realm—are a reflection of me! I can recognize myself in each of them; they now embody my own creativity. As I grow older, I find that I can open myself more to others' energy, which has the advantage of making me bolder. The other, far from being a potential threat, is a convenient mirror.

–Loving Oneself

Over time, I am learning to allow myself happiness and to let my curiosity overcome my once-crippling shyness. This shyness has considerably softened, thanks to yoga and various life events that have pushed me to expand my range of expression.

The practice of yoga changes our emotional state. It leads to the discovery of a profound joy that resides deep within each of us, our true nature. It helps us cultivate self-esteem, self-compassion, encouraging us to stop searching outside for what we are capable of finding within. This discipline can be a powerful tool for transformation.

When I allow my field of awareness to expand, I am given the chance to stop identifying with the image I have of myself, to let go of my identity—at least in these moments of introspection. It feels good to release the narrow definition I have of myself, to realize that we are so much more than our roles in society. No, I am not just a mother, a friend, a teacher, etc.

A certain melancholy took root early on, stemming from the heavy atmosphere of negativity that lingered within the four walls of my childhood, a family tradition of pessimism, as if there were a tacit agreement around the idea that life spares no one. Happiness was almost an offense... There was no room here to blossom in one's uniqueness. How many times did I hear proudly uttered phrases beginning with "I don't like," as if one had to define oneself in the negative. I took on the role of the black sheep early on, not without guilt, since my mother had emphasized my difference and, in doing so, assigned me my role. It suited me in a way, as it seemed to allow me to carve out my own path, but I hadn't realized that I was also obeying a maternal injunction.

One day, I finally understood that anything is possible, at any moment, and that nothing, outside of myself, has the power to limit me. I like to remember that our cells renew themselves every second, and that in this way, we are endlessly given a second chance to reshuffle the card deck!

I had a visceral need for freedom, believing I would lose it if I stopped moving—afraid of becoming frozen in place, like Sleeping Beauty. But ultimately, it was in stillness that freedom revealed itself to me.

−The Power of Life in the Face of Death

A powerful encounter with myself, enabling me to access my authentic story, unfolded through a series of significant events.

In 2003, the passing of my sister marked a profound turning point and the beginning of my deepening interest in spirituality. Until then, I had kept myself in the shadows, but suddenly I felt called to express my full potential. Something greater than myself was urging me to step out of hiding.

Reading *The Audacity to Live* by Arnaud Desjardins helped me climb out of the abyss where my sister's sudden death had plunged me. This book provided the precise definition of the openness I had been seeking all along, stirring within me the call of the unknown. My world felt so small! Desjardins describes the path of yoga as the Ultimate Adventure, revealing the length and difficulty of the journey to fully embrace life. According to him, our fear of death stems from a sense of not truly having lived. It is not death we fear but life itself.

Around this time, I began training to become a yoga teacher and chose the topic of death for my final thesis. I explored how the grief I was experiencing inspired me to embrace life, allowing myself, at last, to live fully.

The call of the unknown sounded even louder in 2015, during my separation from the father of my children. This separation struck me with a muted violence, leaving me stunned. Though it felt like an internal explosion, it also offered me a chance to finally leave the pseudo-secure world of family life. Only later did I realize how much this forced change benefited me.

I was trapped in chronic dissatisfaction that cast shadows over my relationship. I was unable to appreciate the gifts life was offering me. This dissatisfaction stemmed from my choice to remain in the role of a little girl, expecting someone else to heal my childhood wounds. How many of us cling to the idea of a "better half" in adulthood? We fall victim to the romanticized ideal of a couple, perpetuated by our society, deceiving ourselves by giving the other person the keys to our happiness. A relationship built on such foundations is destined to fail.

I continued on my path, journeying alone—too immature to build a solid partnership, too committed to preserving my freedom. Yet, despite my desire for independence, I had granted my partner considerable power and depended financially on him. I lacked the docility that would allow me to believe in the idea of a perfect couple. Meanwhile, a yearning for self-realization had been simmering within me since my sister's passing. As my relationship was unraveling, I glimpsed a new life on the horizon—a fantasy that brought me satisfaction, igniting excitement at the prospect of holding the reins and leaving my own mark on the world.

The Universe offers us trials that disrupt our plans, and we fight against them out of fear of the unknown, not understanding that painful changes can contain the seeds of true treasure. The end of dependency was at hand, but the child within me felt deeply shaken and abandoned, leaving behind 20 years of stability built within a relationship. The insecure little girl resurfaced, crying for help; yet, for the first time, I began to realize that I could comfort and mother her myself. I became aware that the independence I had long dreamed of could, in reality, be achieved by tapping into my own resources, which I had neglected for so long. Why wait for others to provide what we are fully capable of giving ourselves?

At first, however, I retreated into a phase of sadness and fear. I felt unworthy of the spiritual path, paralyzed by guilt. Financial pressures forced me to teach yoga classes back-to-back to make ends meet. Neglecting self-care, I felt more fragmented than ever, at odds with what I was supposed to be teaching. My negativity had begun to regain ground. In 2019, the onset of illness marked a pivotal point. This new chapter compelled me to take charge of the inner child whose emotions had never been met with the tenderness they deserved. Acknowledging our suffering, expressing it without slipping into victimhood, and allowing ourselves the time to experience these unsettling emotions are often neglected steps, cut short in their process.

Illness, in its way, seeks to heal us; it is said that illness is the body's way to seek health. My diagnosis confirmed that my way of functioning was harmful and that a profound change was essential for my survival. The diagnosis was unsurprising, as I knew that different parts of my being were not aligned. In truth, I was blaming myself. Losing my health provided me an opportunity to reconcile with myself.

A kind of liberation began to unfold. Strangely, vast new spaces emerged within me. Instead of restricting or handicapping me, illness became an escape, a way to step outside myself. "To dare to live is to dare to die at each moment, but it's also to dare to be born, to take great steps forward," said Arnaud Desjardins. I immediately accepted the illness and, with it, the gradual need to come to terms with the threat of death. The thought of my own mortality now accompanies me daily, illuminating my path; the instability of my current situation reminds me that life is movement and that constantly seeking security makes existence painful.

Far from being endured as an injustice, this experience allows me to put beauty into perspective. Living this experience is, in a way, extraordinary. The paradox is that this new reality helps me to flourish.

−Solitude and a Return to the Self

With the experience of my family unit breaking apart, which forced me to take a step back, I was led to understand and bring together the different facets of my personality. My soul was no longer reverberating, and illness was a signal of this. A solitary, intimate pause became essential to attempt to decode myself.

This necessary solitude was deepened by a sense of isolation that society often imposes on cancer patients. Since cancer crystallizes fears, we place those affected by it into a realm that feels inaccessible. Suddenly, I found myself on the other side, now among those labeled as "cancer patients." People idealize my courage, though I'm simply trying to adapt as best I can to the situation. I am reflected as a strong person, as if others are attempting to restore a dignity they assume I've lost.

However, I refuse to identify myself with any pathology. Initially, I embarked on a journey of fighting, as it's commonly expected to "fight" to neutralize this invader. But then I realized it wasn't a divine punishment but rather valuable information to welcome and decode. Cancer does not strike randomly.

I strive to reconsider the beliefs society and medicine impose on my fate, despite the invasive imagery surrounding cancer. I feel far more at peace today than in the past and do not envy anyone else's life. I am fortunate not to endure daily pain. Undoubtedly, if I did, it would cloud my perspective on this experience; but for now, it's just uncomfortable enough to shake me from fatalism.

Solitude offers the opportunity to learn to appreciate one's own company. In reality, my solitude becomes sweet when I regain awareness of being part of a Whole. More than ever, I feel the need to strengthen my ties with Nature; my being nourishes itself with its benevolent protection. The forest is like a refuge, cradling me under its maternal wing. "It is a temple," said Baudelaire. Yes, even as a child, it appeared to me as a sanctuary, and my most beautiful childhood memories are found in the wonder of its magic. Nature uplifts.

−The Power of the Present Moment

I have learned to solidify the shelter that the present moment provides. I try not to envision the future, which is primarily structured around the appointments in my treatment schedule. By focusing on the present moment, meditation has taken on profound meaning.

While the episodes of hospitalization have been traumatic, I realized, on a solitary winter evening, that I had the power to console my distress: standing before the terrifying prospect of being cut open once again, I was able to outsmart the scenario my mind was fabricating in anticipation of this event. I recreated, as I did as a child, a space without time, enveloped in the gentle warmth of my sheets, strong in the certainty that the future did not exist here. Only God knew what lay ahead. I then felt at peace, nurtured. I had summoned, in my sleep, protective animals who offered me their assistance.

For I know that if I am in the present moment, I am in eternity. Nothing can happen to me.

3. The Path to Autonomy

Growing up—that is what I have been invited to do in recent years. To access autonomy, it is necessary to become aware of one's dependencies and to question one's framework. What are my true needs? Material comfort has thus taken a back seat. I felt that it encaged me, preventing me from being clear about my priorities.

On the one hand, I became aware that I was living in a rather paternalistic and patriarchal society, having sustained a model of financial dependence on my husband. On the other hand, facing the doctors revealed the little power they granted to patients and their difficulty in looking beyond the physical body. However, healing can only occur through a holistic understanding of the individual, in all its dimensions. How could I limit myself to their strategy of eliminating symptoms, while neglecting to seek their meaning and symbolism? Their authority, often accepted from the start, intimidates patients and inhibits any initiative on their part. They are expected to obey, as if our bodies did not belong to us.

To help me reclaim my sovereignty, I also turned to naturopathy, which focuses on understanding and treating the patient's backdrop alongside the medical management of their symptoms, respecting the body's homeostatic balance. Naturopathy has led me to question all my education regarding nutrition and lifestyle. It has allowed me to recognize my strong dependence on eating habits that are detrimental to my health.

Now more than ever, I believe it is fundamental for me to prioritize my individual freedom over my security. Seeking security keeps us trapped in a paralyzing fear. Yet, paradoxically, I realize how freedom can also be frightening; in recent years, I have come to the surprising realization that we often do not know what to do with it! La Boétie's *Discourse on Voluntary Servitude* emphasizes that there is only oppression if it is voluntary. We create our own tyrants; this is a difficult idea for me to accept, as it reveals our resignation and, thereby, our mediocrity.

My reaction is visceral in situations where I feel pressure is being exerted on me, perhaps because I fear reliving the emotions generated by submission to parental authority. Thus, during the health crisis, I suffered from having to let my actions be dictated to me, without respecting my inner conviction. The herd instinct to which humans, in their animal nature, blindly obey allows governing elites to easily enslave the people. This particularly unique period revealed these widely used mechanisms in our societies and made me understand that we cooperate in the fabrication of this domination. Many questions about my level of submission have agitated me. I could not ignore my immobility and obedience to the restriction on free movement, which undermined a fundamental right. What truly disturbed me was that my deep feelings could not be validated; something in my body did not align with the official version of events. This dissonance between my feelings and what I heard led me to personally analyze the situation, which required me to abandon my trust in the official media, whose narratives sounded false. Until then, I had taken their perspective at face value; now, my quest for truth became responsible and active, and my reevaluation of certain historical events opened surprising horizons for me, teaching me a great deal about the workings of the world and my own filters.

4. Freedom is Responsibility

Self-knowledge and understanding the world around us involve the ability, as adults, to constantly question the beliefs, dogmas, and opinions that have shaped us. This approach liberates us, as it engages our intelligence and personal power, and helps us decondition ourselves. Maintaining a fresh perspective is a constant challenge.

From an early age, I understood that my passivity in situations that called for self-action was my greatest flaw. However, I tended to behave like a child by relying on others. In reality, I needed to seek my own devices and depend less on the help of others. Stepping out of the cocoon requires discipline. Living alone prevents me from transferring my problems onto others. I am responsible for my happiness, and this realization reassures me.

Currently, the booming happiness industry leads many people to follow the guidelines of personal development. Sometimes we lack critical thinking regarding these guides, who are often imagined as the sole holders of Truth, claiming to show us the way. This almost spiritual approach can be confused with a constant search for satisfaction, where the discomfort and pain accompanying life's upheavals are seen as failures. Should we not instead learn to swim in the ponds of our suffering? While the importance of valuing our internal resources and qualities is emphasized in personal development guidance, I lament that caring for our less noble tendencies is not encouraged. Human beings are filled with contradictions; if we are light, we are also cowardice and deceit! There is danger in having to embody the best version of oneself at all costs, as it creates considerable stress. As long as we have not dislodged our darkest feelings and desires and want to present an idealized image of ourselves to the world, we are deceiving ourselves. The danger also lies in the guilt that conceals a form of morality that has permeated mindsets, as shown by the models presented on social media: I am what I choose to show.

In reality, human beings present themselves as if they wanted to belong to team Good. However, the effort they exert in this endeavor is energy-draining, because behind the perfect image they project lies the unconscious expectation for recognition and gratification.

In my view, we are currently subjected to a binary vision that traps us in a singular way of thinking, underpinned by a morality that resembles political correctness. I am now trying to detach myself from this perspective. But it is not easy, as one must accept that the perception of those around us changes when we step off the beaten path of singular thought, a perception that stigmatizes those who stray too far.

The need for belonging to a group and the difficulty of thinking for oneself is also evident in the unconscious loyalty to family, a loyalty that guides us despite ourselves and often plays tricks on us: any attempt to step out of line is guilt-inducing. Uncovering this automatism is, however, a powerful lever for our liberation. Do we ever free ourselves from this loyalty?

Psychoanalyst Alice Miller highlights the danger of a moralizing education that forces us to honor our parents and forgive them even when they have been abusive. We must break free from the omnipotence of our parents because the body does not forget and does not forgive. We must listen to its messages that ensure our integrity. We must confront our childhood traumas at last.

"The body never lies," says Alice Miller. It gives me justice. To stick to the body: it is my compass, my temple, it contains the world.

Now, I discover my responsibility to honor Life, an invaluable gift of which I was unaware. I lived too long in this ignorance. Allowing Life to flow through me has become my only commandment: to acknowledge my fears while opposing them with my faith in life. A sense of gratitude often animates me.

This responsibility to honor Life has created in me a sense of urgency to be; since then, a bubbling energy stirs within me. This exhilaration, born from the realization that my life can end so easily, delays my serenity. I remain in action, yet I am aware of the power of non-action: to travel, to meet, to taste, as if living well consists of accumulating external experiences. I, who until now have been so ungrateful for my incarnation on Earth, still have some time left to marvel. The humility of the flower teaches me to become lighter. It knows how to be content with simply existing.

To always reconnect with the body: meditation occurs through it. To be content with just being means reclaiming one's place, centering oneself in a secure spot within one's existence. To no longer fear death, to leave one's body: the journey is still very long!

To be free, but in my uniqueness, for I have understood that freedom is not to be conquered but cherished, since it is already within me.

"Freedom means letting go. The finite is the price of the infinite, just as mortality is the price of immortality. Spiritual maturity lies in the readiness to let go of everything. Abandonment is the final step. But true abandonment is realizing that there is nothing to let go of, for nothing belongs to you. It is like a deep sleep. You do not abandon your bed when you fall asleep. You forget it." (Nisargadatta Maharaj)

For a long time, I awoke entrapped in my conditioning, weighed down by melancholy, sacrificing my sacred self to conform to a manufactured, reductive image of myself

Yes, we are all called to step up to our potential if we allow ourselves to do so. Today, each new morning is filled with promises, and something very joyful bursts forth within me.

Of course, I must also welcome doubts, fear, and yes, I sometimes waver. But the Yes is always nearby. Melancholy has lost ground.

Céline Pellet

WHAT IF EVERYTHING WERE POSSIBLE?

Holder of a CFC in business administration, I have worked with various companies, including an international one where I held the position of bilingual executive assistant (French/English).

In 2011, I met my spiritual teacher, whose teachings and meditation helped me reconnect with my authenticity. That same year, I decided to pursue training as a therapist in Ayurvedic massage. In 2018, I began training as a practitioner in Ericksonian hypnosis, and in 2020, I embraced the world of intuition.

In my free time, I enjoy walking in the forest to recharge and meditate. An epicurean by nature, I love spending time at the table with the people I care about. My guilty pleasure? Eating black olives while savoring a good glass of red wine. Curious by nature, I enjoy reading books, watching an excellent series, or a great film.

Today, I work part-time in the public sector and practice as a therapist in Nyon, Switzerland.

www.essencedesoi.ch

Instagram - essencedesoi.ch

Céline Pellet

AND WHAT IF EVERYTHING WERE POSSIBLE?

True happiness does not depend on any being, any external object. It depends solely on us...

– Dalai Lama Tenzin Gyatso

First of all, I would like to thank Sophie for allowing me to share with you certain moments from my life, without going into detail, that made me realize the incredible potential we have as human beings, and above all, that hope, love, and faith are key elements for walking our path here on Earth.

My parents' union brought two daughters into the world. From a very young age, I felt different. I felt comfortable with some people and entirely out of place with others. The vibrations I sensed from some were not harmonious but rather unsettling. I share this with you now, but you should know that when I felt all this, I was barely one year old. It was easy for adults to notice my discomfort depending on whose arms I was in.

When I was two and a half, my parents' divorce disrupted my life. I would then grow up alongside my mother and my older sister. After the separation, my mother moved near Lausanne to live with a man and his son. This man was quite unstable in many ways. We experienced all kinds of turmoil. I remember it like it was yesterday—each incident as striking as the next. He would greet my father at the door, brandishing a sword, threatening to stab him if he didn't bring us back on time. His fits of madness would make my stomach knot, and I would often cry. The verbal and physical violence horrified me. One day, my mother washed a small wooden board that ended up cracking, and he flew into a rage, breaking two of my mother's beautiful plates in revenge. Much later, he would spy on my mother, my sister, and me. He left frightening messages on our voicemail, and once he even deflated the tires of the car my aunt had lent to my mother. As you can see, this individual was deeply disturbed, and his madness paralyzed my mother. Taking action had become a risk. However, we all grew attached to his son, who became my lifelong big brother in spirit. He protected, even saved, me and my sister.

One afternoon, as we waited for our mother to go grocery shopping, we were playing in the schoolyard. A man in a motorcyclist outfit appeared out of nowhere and approached my sister. I can still remember his outfit vividly—it was blue and white leather with a bit of black. The motorcyclist started talking to my sister. From a distance, I watched the scene while swaying back-and-forth on my wooden rocking horse. What I saw didn't bode well. Suddenly, a small voice rose within me: "Go to your sister; this man is going to harm her!" Without understanding what was happening, I left my rocking horse and walked toward her.

My heart was pounding, and I was trembling all over. When I drew near, I told her, without understanding why, "You know, we're not supposed to talk to strangers!" But it had no effect. The motorcyclist found a way to manipulate her and, without wasting time, he took her hand. Quickly, I grabbed my sister's other hand. He led us toward the building's entrance. Panic surged inside me, and I began to scream with all my might… and then nothing, black-out. We found ourselves in the basement, in the corridors of the cellar between the bomb shelters. We were terrified, trembling all over. Suddenly, the door opened, and from the shadows emerged light, slowly dispelling the darkness that surrounded us. Our big brother was there; he had heard our screams through the bedroom window and had rushed to our rescue. I will be eternally grateful to him, for without him, who knows what we might have endured. We will never know how many minutes had gone by, and we will always carry a striking memory from that day. A star was watching over us—it was undeniable.

Our mother finally found the courage to leave this man. Life had a wonderful surprise in store for us: A few years later, we would reunite with our brother in spirit, and our paths would never part ways again.

Due to our circumstances, I had to take on responsibilities very quickly because my mother had to work to provide for us, even though my father paid child support. I would make sure to lock and unlock the front door to our house, take care of the household chores, cook, and warm up lunch for my sister and me, and so on. In short, I grew up too quickly, which led me to develop a hypersensitivity that I had to learn to manage throughout my life. In the end, it made me stronger. Even though I wished things would stay the same, I had no choice but to face the changes that life was imposing on me to help me grow.

With nowhere to stay, we moved in with one of my maternal aunts for a few weeks. During that time, I shared a room with two of my cousins. We slept next to each other on two mattresses placed side by side on the floor. Every day, a young girl would watch over us while our mothers were at work. This was the time I discovered "double-sided toast." Breakfast became a daily challenge. How could we avoid getting jam everywhere? Then the situation reversed... My mother found an apartment, and a few months after we moved in, my aunt arrived with her son and daughter. It was their turn to stay with us until they could find their own place.

Around the age of 12, I had to leave my familiar surroundings because our mother remarried and soon became pregnant with a third daughter. This change wasn't easy to understand; I felt it was unfair to move because it would mean changing schools. Leaving my classmates and giving up the athletics group I was part of felt like a loss, only to end up in a small, unfamiliar town. I completed my school year by taking the train back and forth. This small town was vastly different from the Lausanne suburbs I knew. I felt miserable, and loneliness weighed down on me throughout the summer. Puberty was challenging. I felt uncomfortable in my changing body and began to rebel against everything and anything. My father was absent. My sister and I were polar opposites. We didn't spend much time together and often butted heads. We were like cats and dogs, with nothing in common. Fortunately, our relationship has improved over the years!

You may be wondering where my father was during all this time. The answer is simple: He was fighting his own demons, which left me little time with him. We lost touch for most of my childhood and adolescence. My memories with him are limited to the time spent at my paternal grandmother's house in the countryside, surrounded by my beloved cousin, aunt, and uncle.

The dreaded school year arrived, and I was forced to rebuild everything from scratch. I had to work hard to succeed. Deep down, I knew that one day I would land my dream job, and I had to succeed at all costs. Nothing and no one could stop me.

In the end, the move wasn't all bad because with this change of school, I met the person who was going to be my new best friend We spent a lot of time together, chatting and smoking. We were inseparable, each of us rebellious in our own way. Her listening ear was a great comfort to me, although I was unable to do the same for her to prevent her departure. Her presence in my life would be short-lived.

When I was fourteen, my little sister was born. This little bundle of joy was the sunshine in my turbulent adolescence. I cared for her tenderly; she loved to sit on my lap and taste whatever was on my plate, as if it tasted better that way!

In 1999, my best friend was going through a terrible time and had already attempted suicide twice. When I spoke up to ask for help, people thought I was the one with problems. This misunderstanding left me even more alone in the face of her growing pain. In spring of that year, she took her own life, and my world collapsed around me. I felt as if I were living a nightmare. Her death left me devastated, even though it wasn't the first time I had lost someone I loved.

A few years earlier, my godfather had passed away after battling cancer. I remember praying one night in my bed, asking for him to be granted remission. He did experience remission for a little over three years, bringing joy to my fairy godmother. I have beautiful memories of my godfather. I am grateful to have had a few more years to experience his love. My godmother and he instilled in me wonderful human values that I still cherish today.

The loss of my friend threw me off balance. I felt lost and didn't know how to accept the void her death left behind. I often visited my paternal grandmother and spent time with my aunt and uncle. I clung to reading, heavy smoking, and then explored various alternative medicines to help me cope and deal with this grief. At that time, I was doing an apprenticeship in commerce, but I quickly realized that my employer wasn't providing the necessary resources for me to succeed in my training period. Thankfully, after many discussions and with the valuable support of a friend's partner, I managed to redirect my path.

Then, at eighteen and a half, I decided to leave the family nest. A few months earlier, I had met a young woman who became my friend and ended up inviting me to live with her and her two sisters. This new chapter brought me immense inner wealth and stability. I began to feel better after the difficult two years I had just gone through. Despite everything life had thrown my way, my guiding star continued to lead me.

During my apprenticeship, I once had to go to the archives to retrieve some documents, and I noticed handwriting on a cardboard box that I recognized. I couldn't believe my eyes. I asked the secretary, who confirmed that it was indeed my godfather's handwriting, as he had been their accountant years back. Tears welled up, chills ran through my body, and I was deeply moved. I thought to myself, "So, you haven't stopped watching over me from above, have you?" An invisible force was protecting me, and I could not deny it was the truth.

After passing my exams, my professional journey continued. I went on a six-month language study trip and then found a job in a French company specializing in business communication solutions and services. In the meantime, I met a therapist specialized in aura reading. Her words touched my heart and soul, helping me make sense of the different stages of my life.

After a year in this service company, I was wrongfully dismissed. Fortunately, after five months of unemployment benefits, I found a job at a multinational. These ten years allowed me to grow professionally. During this time, I met my spiritual master, Mila Khyentse Rinpoche, a teacher of Tibetan Buddhism and Dzogchen. His teachings and meditation brought me closer to my authentic self. Without knowing it, I was embarking on a journey of transformation, growth, and fulfillment.

Years earlier, my father had tried to come back into my life, but overwhelmed by anger, I had rejected him. It took years for me to accept his silence and abandonment. Thanks to meeting my spiritual master, I began to awaken. During one of his teachings, I understood that at the time of death, we are overwhelmed by our emotions, one of which is regret. In that moment, I realized that I needed to reconnect with my father, open my heart to him, and welcome whatever he had to share. Whether the outcome was positive or not, I didn't want to crucify my father but rather give him a chance, forgive him, forgive myself, and free us both from our respective torments so we could peacefully move forward. Our reunion was intense; we cried and talked. Ultimately, I understood that there are always explanations behind the consequences of our actions.

After my thirtieth birthday, I began training in Ayurvedic massage while continuing to work to support myself. I spent a month in India and returned transformed. I was able to perceive things more and more intuitively and in subtle ways. In 2015, I found a position in the public sector. I continued to invest in my personal development with different training courses. I never stopped—I was thirsty for knowledge. I still didn't fully know where I was heading, but I was heading somewhere.

A pandemic marked the 21st century, beginning in early 2020. That same year, in January, I suddenly lost my godmother. It was a hard blow, entirely unexpected. I knew life was precious and fragile. Time would heal me. I had been by her side as much as I could to support her, and she knew I loved her—that was what mattered most. Also in 2020, in March, my paternal grandmother, my second mother, also passed away. During her life, I had promised to be by her side when the time came. Once again, thanks to my spiritual master's teachings, I was able to watch over her until her last breath, for which I will be eternally grateful. Then, in the summer, my maternal aunt, who was battling cancer, also left us. In November, a terrible tragedy occurred when my best friend's sister was killed in a road accident, and in April 2021, my last grandmother passed away.

Faced with this succession of losses around me, I could have felt crushed or lost my zest for life, but at the same time how could I when countless deaths were being reported worldwide due to this cursed health crisis? Of course, the passing of my loved ones wasn't linked to the pandemic, but it showed me that my experience wasn't unique. By not selfishly turning inward and instead opening myself to the suffering of a world on the brink, I could only love life and humanity more deeply. Accepting that everything can change very quickly leaves room for resilience and wisdom to prevail.

After these events, I understood that meditation had become a lifesaver for me. It anchored me in the present moment, in the here and now, without following the possible agitations of the mind. It's a long process; it requires discipline. The call to meditate grew stronger, and I felt a deep need to retreat completely into my practice. This happened in the spring of 2022.

Upon returning from a six-week solitary meditation retreat, I faced renewed professional tension that would call everything into question. I had to take a break from work to identify the dysfunctional elements, a process that lasted four months. I stopped "doing" to simply "be," to contemplate and move forward more intentionally, to take my time. A therapist friend asked me why I wasn't using the tools I had acquired from my training courses. I thought, "Why not?" I had so many skills. I might as well put them to use! Thank you from the bottom of my heart for your support, my dear—I know you'll recognize yourself in these lines.

A little nod to synchronicity… As I'm sitting here writing these words, you sent me a message on my phone. We are clearly connected to everything, to the universe, and to the divine for some.

I spent some time brainstorming with a friend to find the name for my practice—questions, doubts, a true game of Tetris to put everything together, find the logo, design the website, and so on. In a few months, everything took shape. Thank you, my dear friend; your artistic skills helped me make my dream come true.

Beyond the blessing of walking my path surrounded by wonderful people, the two greatest gifts I received are the support of my family and the magic of life, which never ceases to surprise me. A journey to Bhutan in the spring of 2024 will bring me to the depths of my heart, yours, ours.

Change is an intrinsic condition of our existence. Everything is change, transformation. Accepting this means realizing that anything is possible, that our hearts have untold resources to guide us. Suffering arises when we withdraw, when we resist change. We cannot escape change, no matter what. Happiness is in our hands. It depends on nothing else. We are the creators of our lives, and it is up to us to decide what meaning we want to give them.

Today, I am aware that nothing happens by chance. It's all about synchronicity and karma. I have come to realize my potential, spread my wings, and put my knowledge at the service of guiding others toward listening to their hearts and facing the changes we sometimes fear.

Robert Ischer

TURN YOUR LIFE INTO A DREAM, AND YOUR DREAM INTO REALITY.

Robert Ischer is a Swiss real estate developer and founder of his own company, established in 2018.

With over 20 years of experience in the real estate industry, he has led numerous large-scale projects in French-speaking Switzerland, combining sustainability and innovation.

His company specializes in the development of major, exemplary projects and neighborhoods.

Renowned for his ability to create functional and sustainable spaces, Robert is deeply committed to constructing environmentally friendly buildings, incorporating technologies such as geothermal energy and photovoltaics.

Robert has been married for 20 years to the mother of his two children, aged five and eighteen.

https://www.linkedin.com/in/robert-ischer-immobilier

Robert Ischer

TURN YOUR LIFE INTO A DREAM, AND YOUR DREAM INTO REALITY.

Make of your life a dream, and of a dream, reality.

− Antoine de Saint-Exupéry

DEATH AND REBIRTH

When Sophie reached out to me with the opportunity to contribute to this book, I did not think twice. It was a golden opportunity for me to share my journey—a journey of profound transformation—in the hopes that it would inspire others. I felt that my story, the story of a man who had learned to listen to his inner voice and recognize the signs of synchronicity, would resonate with those at a crossroads in their lives. My aim here is to share my experience so that others see that it is indeed possible to reinvent and radically transform our lives if we learn to trust ourselves and follow the signs.

About six years ago, I made a decision that would upend my life. After ten years at the helm of a family business with a thousand employees, I decided to step down from my position as CEO and embark on a new adventure—one far more uncertain but infinitely more aligned with my deepest aspirations. This decision wasn't easy. It came with doubts, fears, and legitimate concerns but it was necessary. Deep down, I felt that I had to leave everything behind to reinvent myself.

THE BEGINNING

Rewind to ten years ago. At that time, my career seemed like the perfect model of success. I was leading a rapidly growing company, managing large-scale real estate projects. Every day, I navigated high-pressure environments, juggling strategic meetings and complex negotiations with influential clients and demanding business partners. My schedule was packed, every minute calculated and optimized. Colleagues and loved ones saw me as a fulfilled man who had "made it." Financially, I was secure, and socially, I was respected. Yet, inside, I felt a growing emptiness.

This feeling of emptiness, a deep sense of dissatisfaction, began to haunt me more and more. Every morning when I woke up, I heard a little voice telling me, "This isn't the life you want to live." I couldn't explain it clearly, but I knew that despite all appearances of success, something was amiss. I was living a life which, on the surface, was enviable, yet I didn't feel fulfilled. It was as if I were walking in one direction and my soul tugging in another. The most frustrating part was that I couldn't understand where this feeling was coming from.

During that time, I started questioning things: How was it possible to have almost everything one could desire materially and socially, yet still feel such a profound emptiness inside? I didn't have an immediate answer to this question, but I knew something had to give. And it was that little inner voice—the one we all have but often choose to ignore—that pushed me to take the first step toward change.

One day, as I sought to understand what was missing, I stumbled upon a website about hypnosis. It was a subject that, until then, was entirely foreign to me. But something in an article on that website resonated with me. I can't quite explain what drew me to the practice, but my intuition told me I had to explore it. So, I decided to enroll in a hypnosis training course. I still remember the moment I typed "hypnosis Lausanne" into my web browser. I found myself facing a multitude of choices: online courses, coaches, therapists… Which one to choose? I didn't know. But something led me to enroll in an Ericksonian hypnosis training course in Morges[10].

---

[10] *Morges* is a municipality in the *Swiss* canton of Vaud and the seat of the district of *Morges*. The town of *Morges* is situated on Lake Geneva, opposite the majestic Mont Blanc and not far from Lausanne.

It was a purely instinctive choice. I took a week off work to attend the training course without really knowing what to expect. And from the very first days, I felt that this decision was going to change my life.

THE IMPACT OF HYPNOSIS

During that training course, I discovered self-hypnosis, an incredibly powerful tool. I learned to use this technique to dive deeply into myself, to explore my subconscious, and to identify the mental and emotional blocks that were holding me back. It was as if, for the first time, I was connecting with a part of myself that I had long ignored. Self-hypnosis allowed me to piece together the scattered fragments of my identity, to understand why I felt that void, and most importantly, to discover how to fill it.

After that week of training, I returned home with a new perspective on life. But that course was just the beginning of a long inner journey. Over the next three years, I continued to deepen my knowledge of hypnosis and other personal development practices. I read books on meditation, yoga, mindfulness, and took additional courses in hypnosis and self-hypnosis. I wanted to understand what was happening within me and why I felt so disconnected from my life.

Over time, this quest for meaning became an integral part of my daily life. Each day, I dedicated time to exploring my inner world, to meditating, and to practicing self-hypnosis. Gradually, the answers began to emerge. I realized that the life I was living did not align with my core values. I had built a career and a life on foundations that, deep down, did not reflect who I truly was.

TRANSFORMING DAILY LIFE, A PATH FRAUGHT WITH CHALLENGES

If I were to tell you that this process of transformation happened smoothly, I would be lying. In truth, the path toward personal transformation is riddled with obstacles, doubts, and self-questioning. I had to confront deep fears and inner resistances I never imagined even existed.

One of the greatest challenges was reconciling my professional life with this inner quest. With a schedule that remained as busy as ever, finding time to take care of myself—to meditate, to practice self-hypnosis—was a real struggle. But I knew I had to persevere. I knew it was essential for my well-being, even if some aspects of my professional life suffered as a result.

There were also the looks and judgments from others. My colleagues and friends didn't understand what I was doing. To them, it was just a whim, a passing phase. They saw me as someone who had succeeded in everything and couldn't understand why I felt the need to question myself. What is the point of changing when everything is going well?

At first, these criticisms affected me a lot. I doubted myself, I wondered if I was on the right path, but over time, I learned to stop paying attention to others' judgments. I understood that this path was mine and that, even if others didn't understand it, I needed to explore it.

It is important to note that transformation is a gradual process. Don't expect to change everything overnight. If you want to change your life, start with small steps. Take five minutes a day to sit in silence, to breathe deeply, and to reconnect with yourself. Gradually, increase this time. At first it will feel like a constraint but will soon become a habit, and eventually even bring you joy. This is how change occurs: progressively, but sustainably.

THE FIRST SIGNS OF CHANGE

As I moved forward on this path of transformation, signs began to appear around me. These signs, which I would have once ignored or considered mere coincidences, now took on a new meaning. They were messages from the universe, confirmations that I was on the right track.

I remember one particular day when I was giving a speech in front of several hundred people. At the end of my presentation, I improvised and added a quote from *The Little Prince*: "Make of your life a dream, and of a dream, reality." These words came out of my mouth spontaneously, as if they had been placed there by something greater than myself. At the time, I didn't fully understand why I had spoken those words but today, with hindsight, I know it was a sign—a sign that something deeper was happening within me.

That day, I realized I had to make a choice. I had to choose between continuing the comfortable yet unsatisfying path I already knew, or dare to leave everything behind and follow my instincts. It wasn't an easy decision to make. There were long nights of insomnia, endless discussions with myself, moments of doubt and fear. But in the end, I chose to trust. I chose to listen to that little inner voice that told me to leave my position as CEO and venture into the unknown.

LEAPING INTO THE UNKNOWN

Making the decision to leave such a prestigious and comfortable position wasn't easy. Leaving behind a secure career, a substantial salary, and a respectable position of power to dive into the unknown was frightening, but something deep within me said it was the right thing to do. That little inner voice, the one I had learned to listen to, urged me to take that step and to not let fear hold me back.

The day I announced my resignation, I felt a mix of terror and liberation. I was jumping into the void without knowing where I would land, but very quickly, that void was filled with a new euphoria. For the first time in years, I felt truly free—free to choose my path, free to create, free to dream.

The first few days after leaving my job were strange. I was alone with myself, no overloaded agenda, no meetings, no incessant phone calls. It was an overwhelming silence, but also deeply soothing. I finally had the space to think, to redefine my priorities, to consider what I truly wanted to do with my life.

Of course, doubts returned. The fear of failure manifested itself several times. After all, I had left an enviable position to embark on a project that, at the time, was still vague. But I continued to listen to that little inner voice, the one that had guided me this far, and gradually, the doubts began to fade.

BUILDING SOMETHING NEW

Once the initial worries dissipated, I began to feel a deep satisfaction in building something new, with my own two hands: creating my own real estate development office, developing my own projects, working according to my values and at my own pace—all of this brought me a joy I had never known before. Every small success, every signed contract, every new client was a victory that felt even more rewarding because it resulted from my own choices.

This process of creation allowed me to rediscover aspects of myself I had long ignored. In a large company, it is easy to conform to a role, to an image, but as an entrepreneur, I was able to redefine my priorities, reconnect with my passions, and above all, rediscover the joy of dreaming and reimagining what I truly wanted for my life.

SYNCHRONICITY AND SIGNS

Throughout this process of transformation, I learned to pay attention to signs—to those events that one could easily dismiss as "coincidences" but which, for me, are much more than that. They are signs that the Universe places on our path to guide us, to show us that we are on the right track.

For example, on several occasions, I thought of someone I hadn't seen in a long time and then ran into them shortly thereafter. Or I regularly saw the time "11:11" on my phone, my computer, or clocks. These are small signs, small nods from the Universe, but they are important. They remind us that we are not alone and that we are supported in our journey.

By learning to listen to these signs and to trust my intuitions, I was able to make decisions more in line with my deepest needs. These synchronicities allowed me to seize unexpected opportunities, avoid certain mistakes, and above all, feel more in tune with the path I was taking.

Let me share three concrete examples of synchronicity in my life over the past eighteen months:

THE SMALL WOODEN TABLE WITH GOLDEN EDGES

For several months, I worked in a small, shared office where I had only a few square meters at my disposal. I felt stuck, unable to move forward, and the space in which I worked contributed to this feeling of suffocation. I was seriously considering changing environments but didn't dare take the step.

One day, while thinking about an architect I knew and hadn't seen in a long time, I ran into her by chance on the street.

We agreed to meet a few days later at her office. During our meeting, a small wooden table caught my attention. I asked her where she had bought it, and she offered to give it to me because she was moving to new premises.

A few months later, I was able to move into the architect's office—a bright and inspiring space where I have since hired three people to contribute to this new stage of my adventure. This change would have been unimaginable eighteen months ago. What a beautiful synchronicity!

The small wooden table with golden edges is now in my office. The golden edges symbolize the transformation of an ordinary object into something extraordinary. They are an invitation to look beyond the functionality of an object, to appreciate the details that can make simple things unique.

Such synchronicity can be interpreted as a reminder to mind the details in daily life, to find beauty in the ordinary, and to turn simple moments into invitations for something memorable and precious.

THE CALL OF THE FOREST

During a trip to Barcelona, I felt irresistibly drawn to the Basilica of the Sagrada Família[11]. It wasn't just a desire to visit a tourist

---

[11] The **Basílica i Temple Expiatori de la Sagrada Família** is a church under construction in the Eixample district of Barcelona, Catalonia, Spain. It is the largest unfinished Catholic church in the world. Designed by Catalan architect Antoni

attraction in a foreign city but rather an inner calling. Looking back, I would almost dare to say that the basilica itself summoned me for a long weekend in Barcelona so that I could have an encounter with it. Entering the building feels like stepping into a natural cathedral, where the stone seems to breathe, move, and grow like a majestic forest. The silence that reigns is reminiscent of that deep within a forest. This silence is not empty but filled with a subtle energy, a living presence, like being in the woods, where one can sense the rustling of leaves, the whisper of the wind, or the songs of birds. The light, omnipresent yet filtering through the branches of the intertwining columns, evokes the light that shines through the leaves of a tree, offering both a sense of protection and an opening toward the sky. In that moment, I rediscovered the magic of my childhood. This experience reminded me of the importance of taking the time to (re)connect with nature and the wonders it offers us.

As I write these lines, I know I must return so that the grand and beautiful mineral forest of Barcelona can teach me something new. I'm off to book my tickets for another pilgrimage!

THE RAINBOW

One day, after losing two major contracts, I felt discouraged. It seemed like everything was going wrong, and the efforts I had invested were bearing no fruit. On my way home, driving through

Gaudí (1852–1926), in 2005 his work on Sagrada Família was added to an existing (1984) UNESCO World Heritage Site, "Works of Antoni Gaudí".

heavy rain, I inwardly asked for a sign, something that would restore my hope. At that moment, as I took the highway exit leading to my house, an enormous, bright rainbow appeared before me. Rainbows emerge after a storm and are symbolically linked to the idea of renewal and hope. After difficult or chaotic times, they are reminders that light and beauty can still emerge. Even after the darkest moments, there is always the potential for light and rebirth. This rainbow encouraged me to stay in the present moment because rainbows vanish as quickly as they appear. It invited me to mindfulness, to savor without filters the instant when beauty becomes manifest. I took it as an invitation to express gratitude and to acknowledge the importance of taking the time to appreciate the wonders that surround us, even if they are temporary. I arrived home that evening with my heart full of light and hope!

I could share countless other examples with you, but I have chosen these three because they stood out to me as stories that belonged in this book. I hope they inspire you and help you become more attentive to the signs you encounter in your everyday life.

WHAT NOW?

If I could give you just one piece of advice today, it would be this: Do not be afraid. Do not be afraid to listen to that small inner voice urging you to change, to reinvent yourself. Trust yourself and follow the signs that life places in your path. These signs are there to show you that you are on the right track, even if the way forward seems uncertain. Yes, there will be obstacles, doubts, and moments of discouragement, but the reward is immense. The reward is the feeling of living a life that truly reflects who you are, a life that has meaning.

"And now here is my secret. It is very simple: One sees clearly only with the heart. That which is essential is invisible to the eyes."

Brigitte Bojkowszky

FROM HIDING
TO THRIVING

Brigitte Bojkowszky is a visionary Brand Identity Strategist and Business Educator with decades of global expertise in crafting transformative and impactful brand identities. A trusted partner to both organizations and individuals, she specializes in holistic branding—reshaping corporate brands, aligning cultures with values, and defining entrepreneurial and leadership identities.

From her early career as a flight attendant to corporate leadership, academia, and ultimately entrepreneurship, Brigitte brings a wealth of experience and a proven track record of success. Her unique journey fuels her ability to connect deeply with her clients, helping them uncover their unique brilliance and step into their full potential with confidence and clarity.

Dedicated to serving a higher purpose, Brigitte is passionate about empowering corporations and individuals to see their own greatness and embrace it. Through her work, she inspires her clients to align their inner values with their outward expression, fostering authentic, impactful brands that leave a lasting impression.

My contacts:

Website BridgetBrands: https://www.bridgetbrands.com
LinkedIn: https://www.linkedin.com/in/bojkowszkyb/

Brigitte Bojkowszky

FROM HIDING TO THRIVING: MY JOURNEY OF BECOMING VISIBLE

The moment you doubt whether you can fly, you cease forever to be able to do it.

– J.M. Barrie, Peter Pan

For years, I lived in the shadow of a traumatic event that could have taken my life. I was a victim of a murder attempt, and the fear of that man returning to silence me forced me into hiding—not just physically, but emotionally and spiritually. I silenced myself, believing I didn't deserve to be seen or heard, and certainly not to thrive. Inside me was a constant battle: one side longed to live boldly, to embrace life's fullest potential, while the other side whispered that I was unworthy, too much for this world, not good enough, not worth the space I occupied. For 35 years, this struggle was my reality.

Today, I am healing. I am on a journey from invisibility to visibility, from self-denial to self-acceptance. I am learning to own my strengths, embrace my flaws, and shine in my uniqueness. I learned to trust that I survived for a reason: to make an impact and to leave the world a little better than when I arrived. I believe we all have a mission in life, a purpose that calls to us the moment we are born. The challenge lies in becoming aware of it—a journey that is often far from easy.

THE UNCONVENTIONAL PATH: FROM THE SKIES TO THE CLASSROOM

Reflecting on my journey—from flight attendant to student, corporate employee, professor, and finally, solopreneur—I see a path that has been anything but traditional. Each twist and turn, every job, and every moment of uncertainty has shaped who I am today. My intuition has been my guiding light, pulling me through even when the road was rocky. The pieces of my story—each experience and hardship—have refined my character, sharpened my skills, and led me to discover my true purpose.

My journey began at 36,000 feet above the ground as a head flight attendant, where I cultivated leadership skills and an appreciation for diverse cultures. I thrived in the skies, mastering the art of creating exceptional experiences, and learning the true value of detail and customer-centricity. It was there, among the clouds, that my passion for brand excellence took root. From Bangkok to Sydney, and across to Cancun, the Caribbean Islands, LA, and Miami, I lived a life filled with rich, cultural encounters that made the world feel like a connected and colorful place. I absorbed different ways of life and behaviors, embedding them into my own identity. Yet, these experiences also distanced me from my traditional Austrian roots, making me feel like an outsider.

Despite the glamorous life of high-end hotels and world travel, I found myself yearning for more intellectual stimulation. I knew that my time in the skies was limited; our contracts would end automatically by the age of 36, leaving me at a crossroads. The decision to leave this adventurous life was one of the hardest but most necessary transitions I've ever made. With no option to study while flying, I chose to pursue higher education—a Master's in Business Education and International Marketing Management. The shift from flight attendant to student was daunting. I faced self-doubt, wondering if I was smart enough to pass the exams. Even one of my professors, judging me solely on my blonde hair and flight attendant background, doubted my potential, convinced I wouldn't make it. But I was determined to prove her wrong—and I did.

I aimed to return to the aviation industry, aspiring to climb the corporate ladder. This vision drove me through 4.5 challenging years of study, including semesters abroad at UCLA in the US and Nanyang University in Singapore and a 3-months internship in India. Living off my savings from flying was tough, but I was fueled by my ambition. However, upon graduation, I was confronted with a harsh reality: the airline industry was in turmoil, and my dream of returning to aviation was no longer feasible. Faced with the need to pivot, I turned within the private sector, taking roles in various industries, only to feel an unshakeable sense that something was missing.

Then, I stumbled upon a newspaper ad for a research and teaching assistant position at the Vienna University of Economics and Business (WU-Vienna), which called to me like a beacon. Out of 100 applicants, I was chosen, and this opportunity became the next pivotal moment in my life. It allowed me to pursue a Doctorate in International Marketing & Management, solidifying my commitment to continuous growth and learning. My academic journey took me across the globe again, to UMSL in Missouri, to teach International Management as a visiting professor for one school year bearing in mind to return to Austria and pursue a career in corporate.

Eventually, I was exploring corporate roles in the real estate development sector. However, life has a way of shaking things up. The 2008 financial crisis hit, and I suddenly found myself without a job. This setback became a turning point, forcing me to reevaluate my path. It was then that I realized the importance of cultivating a personal brand – being aware of your own identity that was independent of any company or external validation. Rather than wallow in self-pity, I saw this as an opportunity to redefine myself. I invested my time in earning a certification as a leadership trainer, focusing on building skills that would not only empower me but also allow me to guide others.

CONFRONTING THE INNER CONFLICT

While contemplating my next steps, the dean of international studies at WU-Vienna invited me to expand my teaching role of just teaching as a sideline. Embracing the opportunity, I shifted fully into academia, merging my corporate experience with teaching. This new path allowed me to blend real-world insights with academic rigor, deepening my credibility and fueling my passion for empowering others. I taught at universities across Austria and took on international assignments in Canada, Russia, China, Vietnam, and more. Each experience broadened my perspective, but beneath the professional achievements, a familiar internal conflict simmered.

Despite my expertise, I felt constrained, and silenced by academic traditions that dulled my creativity and stifled my voice. I had built a life around expectations that left no room for my vision, playing small and molding myself to fit a role that wasn't truly mine. The dissonance between who I was and who I aspired to be echoed the lifelong trauma of feeling unworthy—an internal battle that had shadowed me since childhood. Growing up, I was constantly told we were "not good enough," and taught to stay quiet and remain unseen, a narrative that kept me from thriving.

So I did just that. I silenced my dreams and ambitions, convincing myself that I didn't deserve to stand out. But the desire to break free was relentless. I had always dreamed of venturing out on my own, becoming my own boss, and guiding diverse organizations—from corporations to startups—by bringing an outside perspective that could ignite change and drive impact. I yearned to work with leaders, teams, and individuals, the very pillars that sustain these corporate entities, helping them reach their full potential.

Yet, my internal struggle persisted. The university had made it clear: There was no career path for me. As a teaching professor, I was confined by a system that stifled growth and offered no room for elevation. This went against my conviction to continuously evolve and pursue personal development. I felt trapped by a ceiling I couldn't break through.

One day, I realized the comfort zone I clung to had long stopped being comfortable. The routine lacked joy, the kind that makes life feel light and vibrant. Isn't it true that unconditional happiness is one of life's most vital pursuits? I recognized that stability was an illusion; the only constant is change.

With that realization, I made the decision to leap into the unknown and finally pursue what I had always envisioned: becoming my own boss.

THE PATH TO ENTREPRENEURSHIP: EMBRACING VISIBILITY

Shedding the constraints of my academic identity, I stepped boldly into entrepreneurship. The shift was liberating. For the first time in years, I felt truly alive, aligned with my purpose, and unburdened by the expectations that once held me back. I was no longer living a life dictated by others; I was finally living on my own terms.

Choosing the path of a solopreneur was anything but easy. I faced rejection after rejection, felt unseen by companies, and endured years of uncertainty that would have made many give up. But my calling was louder than my doubts. My parents, though apprehensive, supported me because they understood that my passion was something neither they nor anyone else could steer me away from. The only way was forward; I had to keep showing up, as there was no going back.

When I made the transition, everything changed, both professionally and personally. I let go of many people—friends who were more like acquaintances, those who drained my energy instead of fueling it. To me, friendship is about trust, uplifting one another, and finding joy even in difficult times. I distanced myself from people in my inner circle who no longer aligned with the person I was becoming. I embraced solitude for a couple of years, allowing myself the space to reconnect with who I truly am. During this time,

I surrounded myself only with those who brought positivity into my life. This period of introspection opened me up to receive, and I began to cultivate new, lifelong friendships with individuals who fueled my life with meaningful perspectives.

These changes pushed me to a new level. They provided the clarity I needed to elevate, leap forward, and integrate new insights into my journey. My vision became sharper, my goals more defined, and I found the strength to pursue them on a higher plane.

Looking back on my unconventional path—a journey that was far from linear—I now see it as a puzzle that finally fits. Every stage, every setback, and every step contributed to the bigger picture. From flight attendant to student to corporate to teaching professor to entrepreneur, my diverse experiences have shaped me into a creator of identities and exceptional experiences, preparing me for this moment.

LESSONS LEARNED ALONG THE WAY

Every step of my journey was worth its time, pace, and space, helping to build the foundation for the next chapters in my life. I am now committed to serving and creating for the higher good, as a leader who sees others' greatness and helps them see their own.

1.   Trust your intuition and reflect regularly:

Your intuition is more than just a fleeting feeling—it's your inner compass, guiding you through the complexities of life, especially when the path ahead is uncertain. Regular self-reflection is key to deepening this connection, offering the space to reconnect with your values and recalibrate your choices. By listening to this inner voice and creating moments of stillness, you honor your true self. It's in these moments of introspection that you find clarity, gain perspective, and muster the courage to follow your own unique path.

2.   Stay true to your core values:

Your core values are the principles that define you, the anchors that keep you grounded when life feels turbulent. They guide you through difficult choices and external pressures, ensuring you act with integrity and authenticity. In a world that constantly pushes conformity, staying true to your values helps you live a life that is honest, fulfilling, and uniquely yours. These values are your steady foundation, silently supporting you toward the life that feels right for you.

3.   Don't take others' judgments personally:

The judgments of others often say more about them than about you. When people attempt to diminish your worth, it's usually a reflection of their own fears, insecurities, and unmet aspirations.

Your courage, resilience, and authenticity can be a mirror highlighting what they lack within themselves. So, do not let their words weigh you down. Remember, you are not defined by their opinions but by your own sense of self. Stand firm in your truth, and let your inner strength shield you from the negativity of others.

4.   Being invisible is a disservice to the world:

Each of us carries a unique set of gifts, talents, and perspectives that are meant to be shared. When you hide your light, you deprive the world of your unique contributions and the impact only you can make. You have something special to offer, whether it's your ideas, your voice, or your ability to inspire others. By choosing to remain unseen, you hold back the potential to influence and uplift. Step boldly into your own light, because your presence, your story, and your impact are needed now more than ever.

5.   Be selective about whose advice you take:

Not all advice is created equal. While many people will offer their opinions, not everyone will understand the intricacies of your journey or the challenges you face. Seek guidance from those who have walked a similar path or who genuinely understand your aspirations. Unsolicited advice from those who lack insight into your journey can be misleading and counterproductive. Trust your own wisdom first and surround yourself with mentors and advisors who align with your values and vision.

6. You are not a failure; you are on your path:

Success is not a linear journey; it is an ongoing process of growth, discovery, and resilience. Every setback, every detour, and every so-called failure is simply a part of your unique path. Where you are now is not a measure of your worth or potential but a step in your evolving story. Embrace the journey, knowing that each challenge equips you with the lessons needed for the next phase of your life. You are not behind; you are exactly where you need to be to become who you are meant to be.

7. Dare to dream BIG:

Dreams are the seeds of our future, and the only limits placed upon them are the ones we impose on ourselves. Do not allow the doubts of others or the fears within you to shrink your vision. Dream as boldly and as expansively as you dare and take deliberate steps toward making those dreams a reality. The world needs your audacious dreams, your daring vision, and your courage to pursue the impossible. Remember, the only true barrier is the belief that you can't; everything else is just a hurdle to be overcome.

8. Know your WORTH:

You are inherently deserving of all the success, respect, and joy that life has to offer. Your worth is not contingent upon external validation or the approval of others; it resides within you. When you recognize your own value, you set the standard for how others should treat you. Do not settle for anything less than what aligns with your worth, whether in your career, relationships, or any area of your life. Surround yourself with people who recognize your value, uplift your spirit, and respect your journey.

9. Embrace the journey, not just the destination:

Life is not just about reaching a final destination; it's about the experiences, the growth, and the lessons learned along the way. Embrace the highs and lows, the successes and setbacks, for they all shape who you are becoming. Every moment is an opportunity to learn, evolve, and deepen your understanding of yourself. The journey itself is rich with meaning, and it's in the process of becoming that we find our true selves. Celebrate each step forward, for it's all part of the beautiful tapestry of your life.

10. Have joy in life: What is a life without joy?

Moments of joy are what give life its sparkle. They are the precious, unforgettable experiences that add richness to our days—whether spent alone, with dear friends, or even shared with strangers who, in a fleeting instant, change the course of our lives. Sometimes, it's the unexpected magic of an ordinary moment that becomes extraordinary. Joy doesn't have to be grand; it can be found in the simple, everyday occurrences that light up our hearts. Embrace these moments, for they are the true gems of life, reminding us why we strive, persevere, and love.

Finding my purpose didn't happen overnight; it took years of unlearning old beliefs, listening to my intuition, and daring to be visible. But the journey is worth it. I now live my truth, not because it's easy, but because it's mine. And I'm here to tell you— so can you.

CRAFTING YOUR TRUE IDENTITY

Branding starts with mindset.

– Brigitte Bojkowszky

When people think of branding, they often associate it with companies, products, or services. But branding goes beyond corporate logos and catchy slogans—it applies to us as individuals. Personal branding is about how we present ourselves to the world. It's the identity we project, the perceptions we shape in others' minds through our appearance, attitudes, behaviors, and actions.

The truth is, whether we realize it or not, we are always communicating our brand to the world. And if we aren't intentional about it, others will be. Why let others define us? Why hand over the power to shape our identity to someone who doesn't truly know us? Personal branding is not about constructing a façade but about giving ourselves permission to be unapologetically authentic. It's about owning who we are and living in alignment with our true self, from a place of humility and confidence.

EMBRACING THE FUTURE: LIVING MY VISION

As I move forward, I am guided by a clear vision—my North Star. It's not just about goals; it's about living a life aligned with my core values, a life that reflects who I truly am. I have so many aspirations, but two stand out on my wish list—one professional and one personal.

On my personal bucket list is an experience that symbolizes freedom: skydiving. Jumping from a plane, feeling the rush of wind, and embracing the thrill of the fall—it's more than just an adrenaline rush. For me, it's a metaphor for letting go of control, trusting the process, and fully embracing the unknown. It's a physical manifestation of my journey of becoming visible, of living boldly and without fear.

Professionally, I am working towards building a brand centered around empowering others to find their voice, own their narrative, and thrive on their terms. My vision includes hosting exclusive branding retreats at luxury, secluded spas and resorts—spaces that embody my commitment to quality and excellence. These retreats will blend my passions for traveling, teaching, and creating meaningful communities, reflecting the journey I've lived so far. Through this, I aim to inspire others to step into their full potential, to be seen, heard, and unafraid to shine.

FINAL THOUGHTS

I've learned to trust my intuition, embrace change, and, most importantly, define success on my own terms. My story is a testament to the power of resilience, adaptability, and the courage to pursue a path that's uniquely mine. I am committed to continuous growth, not because it's easy, but because it's the only way to honor the person I am becoming. And through it all, I have learned that the most valuable brand I will ever build is the one that starts from within.

The journey to visibility is ongoing. It's not about reaching a final destination but about continuously showing up as your authentic self. Each day, I strive to embrace my story, own my worth, and live a life that's true to who I am. I hope my story inspires you to do the same.

Dr. Brigitte Bojkowszky

Guillaume Collignon

LISTEN TO YOUR HEART

Curious about new experiences, sensations, and challenges, I enjoy trying out numerous sports, often labeled as extreme, and driving or piloting any mode of transportation that comes my way.

Through all of this, I've scared myself (often), hurt myself (a few times), but most importantly, I've enjoyed myself (every single time) and, above all, felt alive.

Stepping out of one's comfort zone can be intimidating, stressful, even frightening, but it opens us up to so many new possibilities, horizons, and skills that free us from the cocoon we create and then impose upon ourselves.

It would be a shame to miss out on an undiscovered passion or an enriching activity because of barriers we build for ourselves.

They say facing your fears is the definition of courage. I don't entirely agree. We never truly know what will happen, so why be defeatist in advance? Why not dive into the unknown? And most of all, why fear the unknown?

That's my philosophy: Before forbidding yourself from doing something, you have to try it first.

Guillaume Collignon

LISTEN TO YOUR HEART

Truth is found in simplicity.

– Attributed to Isaac Newton.

I have always found it difficult to talk about myself. I don't like to be in the spotlight and prefer discretion and anonymity. If someone doesn't remember having crossed paths with me, I'm perfectly fine with that. Despite this characteristic of mine, I'm going to attempt to tell you my humble story and life's coincidences that led me to make some career changes.

Perhaps we can say that I've often lacked foresight, but the fact is that I never anticipated the events that shaped my choices; they have always been a response to a change in circumstances. So, I will endeavor to recount my professional wanderings in fields that are worlds apart from one another.

After many doubts about which path to embark on for my studies—wavering among accounting, sales, and management—

I eventually decided to pursue a degree in tourism. I was quick to imagine my future, traveling the world, gaining experiences abroad, and leading an exciting life.

In 1997, I was hired by a travel agency in Annecy[12], specialized in business trips. Despite a few "educational" trips, my daily life consisted of sitting in an open space, eyes staring at my computer, and the phone glued to my ear. Although I had thought I would be exploring the world by working at a travel agency, my job turned out to be sedentary. Fortunately, I was surrounded by pleasant colleagues who brightened my workdays, as the job became increasingly tedious, with ever-growing pressure year after year.

The 2001 attacks and their impact on air traffic followed by the rise of online booking sites for travelers began to render my profession obsolete. Travel agencies were closing down one after another, and the one I worked for was no exception. I was offered a managerial position at another agency in northern France. I had seen the movie *Bienvenue Chez les Ch'tis*[13] (*Welcome to the Sticks*) and greatly enjoyed it, but that's as far as it goes. There was no

---

[12] Annecy is a picturesque town in southeastern France, situated near the French Alps and is known for its stunning lake.

[13] *Bienvenue chez les Ch'tis* (*Welcome to the Sticks* in English) is a popular 2008 French comedy film directed by Dany Boon. The story follows a postal worker from southern France who is transferred to a small town in the northern region, known for its distinct culture and strong regional accent. Initially dreading the move, he eventually discovers the warmth and humor of the local people, challenging stereotypes about life in northern France.

way I was moving to the North. I had no choice but to look for a different career.

In January 2009, just days after leaving the agency, as I was pondering my career change, I saw an ambulance speeding by, sirens blaring and blue lights flashing all around. I thought to myself, 'It must be "cool" to be an ambulance driver and do that for a living.'

After some research, I learned a bit more about this profession, which seemed fascinating to me. I increasingly felt the urge to give it a try and dive into this new career path.

In early June, I started training to obtain the state-certified ambulance driver's diploma. My studies would last six months, alternating between classes and internships. I had moments of doubt mixed in with exhilarating experiences. However, my inexperience allowed me to learn without questioning the education I was receiving. In the end, I surprised myself because I realized that I enjoyed learning—something that, unfortunately, wasn't the case during my university studies.

In November 2009, I finally became a certified ambulance driver. After 12 years spent inside an office, staring at a computer screen, I would finally be outdoors, feeling emotions, experiencing sensations, and getting my daily dose of adrenaline. In short: I was going to have a blast!

Then November 2021 came around and, well, a blast is what I had… I fell from the height of one story to the bottom of a flight of stairs, and it hurt, which means I'm still alive. I struggled to get up, my right hand covered in blood, my finger badly cut. My pants were torn on the right side and my right leg was soaked in blood. The worst of all was that I could no longer walk on my left foot without the sting of intense pain, a sign that didn't bode well.

But this wasn't the time to feel sorry for myself. I had a patient to transport to a medical appointment, so I handed the ambulance keys to my colleague.

Once at the hospital, I used the stretcher as a walker. That way, I could complete my task properly before heading back to the company to gather my things and my car, and then make my own way to the emergency room. It was tough using the clutch, but I was determined to stay independent, so I gritted my teeth.

After a consultation with an emergency doctor whom I completely trusted, I ended up with four stitches on my finger, the same on my leg, and a broken foot, along with a sick leave—the very first one in my life.

MANDATORY REST

After ten days of not working, I went for a follow-up X-ray. Despite the persistent pain, I was hopeful. Being stuck at home was driving me crazy and I missed running, cycling, and hiking in the mountains.

Unfortunately, the verdict was undeniable: the doctors found an avulsion fracture that had gone undetected in the ER. My doctor extended my leave for another month.

I had a bad feeling about the future of my career, and even worse for my favorite outdoor activities. One month after, another follow-up X-ray only confirmed my fears: the fracture had not healed, and what was more, the small bone fragment was moving and regularly hitting a nerve, which explained the sharp pains I sometimes felt.

TIME TO OPEN A NEW CHAPTER

"You will need to reconsider your professional future," said the medical advisor at Social Security, who shared the same assessment as my regular physician. It had now been over three months since I was off work. The stubborn fracture refused to heal, and it seemed that it would be permanent.

But what to do? I could no longer have a 'physical' job, I didn't want to go back to an office job, and I wanted to use my knowledge in first aid. During a family meal, I learned that one of my cousins had switched careers a few years ago to become a first aid trainer. Why not take inspiration from his experience?

The very next day, I contacted him, and our conversation filled me with a lot of hope. My profile seemed to fit this field. The technical side didn't scare me; however, the teaching side was another story.

A few weeks later, the training course to become a safety instructor began. Technically, I felt comfortable. The teaching aspect was a bit more complicated, but I was making steady progress.

That said, I had forgotten to consider the essential mastery of IT tools, and that was extremely challenging. Fortunately, I was well-supported, which allowed me to successfully complete the exams.

Not being very confident about this career change, I resumed working part-time as an ambulance driver but I wasn't very motivated. I no longer felt as though as I was in my element, which was very unsettling and anxiety-inducing.

STEPPING INTO THE UNKNOWN

A year later, after making the decision to leave my job and dive into the unknown, I started working as a freelancer.

Since I wasn't alone in my new field of first aid training, my first assignments didn't come until two months later.

After spending the weekend before my first lesson in a state of considerable apprehension, I found myself in front of a class filled with people from a range of different backgrounds who were all completely new to first aid. I felt the pressure rise because I was afraid I wouldn't be able to meet their expectations and would disappoint them. But I quickly realized that I was facing an attentive and supportive audience. Ultimately, the first class went well, and I took immense pleasure in sharing my experience and sharing my knowledge. It was a true revelation.

The following classes reassured me in my choice, although it was sometimes challenging to capture the attention of some people, regardless of their age, profession, or responsibilities. But as soon as I introduced the CPR module, I gained everyone's focus, and group cohesion started to take shape.

I never thought my job was extraordinary. When friends ask me about my experiences as an ambulance driver, their eyes open wide in astonishment when I tell them about the variety of things I had to do: perform cardiac massages, assess a patient's condition so the hospital team can suitably prepare for admittance, reassure family about a patient's condition, calm down a hysterical person, call law enforcement in case of a threat, and even the intense experience of delivering a baby. This job had me facing both life and death, with all the nuances of emergencies in between. If my career had any logic, some would call it synchronicity, and they know who they are. Indeed, there was a degree of synchronicity that allowed me to nourish my new role as a first aid trainer with my past knowledge and experiences.

Why did I wait so long to pursue a profession that didn't encroach on my personal life and which brought me so much satisfaction? The security and convenience of a stable job are not guarantees of personal fulfillment.

This career change was a liberation and an achievement, and I encourage you all to take the leap if your profession brings you no joy.

Life is too short, enjoy it!

Claire-Lise Botteron

THE MAGIC OF THE PRESENT MOMENT

Passionate about movement, synchronicities, and life's offerings, Claire-Lise dances with it all, embracing a vision open to renewal.

Espace Mouvements de vie is the name she chose for her healing space. Naturally kinesthetic, she has always placed great importance on the body in motion. It was through bodily practices that she began her journey into personal development. This same joy of touch led her to practice massage. She has trained in various manual and energetic techniques, offering treatments tailored to each individual's needs.

Her vision is to create a space of support and exchange, aligned with each person's aspirations for change and transformation.

In *Daring Metamorphoses*, Claire-Lise shares her wonder at the diverse ways life answers our paths, offering readers confidence and openness toward those responses.

Join Claire-Lise in her adventures, where only movement can carve the way forward.

Facebook : Claire-Lise Botteron

Facebook Page : Espace Mouvements de vie

Claire-Lise Botteron

THE MAGIC OF THE PRESENT MOMENT

If you think adventure is dangerous, try routine; it is lethal.

− Paulo Coelho

Being in the present moment, immersed in joy, gratitude, enthusiasm, and wonder, with the lightheartedness of a child, elevates me to a vibration that attracts the best for me in that moment and fulfills my needs.

At fifteen, I started an apprenticeship in confectionery and pastry-making. With my father's help, I found a position in the charming little town of Vevey, Switzerland over 100 kilometers from home. At that time, there weren't enough apprenticeship opportunities offering sandwich courses, and none were available in my region.

It was a major change—I had to rent a room far from my family and friends and adapt to a professional life surrounded mostly by men. The days started early in the morning, and weekends were the busiest.

I had a knack for the craft, which I enjoyed, but the work environment was absolutely awful. My boss was irritable, shouting and cursing all day long. I am naturally a calm and sensitive person so this atmosphere didn't suit me at all. I would go to work with a knot in my stomach, wishing I'd fall ill just to have an excuse to escape it all. My parents realized something was wrong, came to pick me up, and made arrangements so I wouldn't have to return.

Back home, I had to find a new placement since I was just beginning my second year of a three-year apprenticeship. We were friends with the village baker, so we asked if he knew of any confectioneries looking for an apprentice. He referred us to a confectioner in the area. We visited him, but he didn't have an opening although perhaps his brother-in-law, who also owned a confectionery in Lausanne, might. The answer was yes!

It was perfect for me because this confectionery was in the same canton as my previous placement, which meant I could continue my education at the same school. After a one-week break between the two jobs, I resumed my apprenticeship in a much better environment and was met with great success—I graduated second in my class.

Backed by my good results, I found a job in a confectionery closer to my family and hometown. I passed my driving test, rented a small apartment, and officially entered adulthood.

The work hours were still grueling. Mornings began between four and six o'clock, evenings ended whenever the work was done, and weekends were fully occupied. On top of this, the work environment was unpleasant. Nevertheless, I loved what I did and pushed through. But living my young adult life under these conditions was challenging. The general atmosphere at the confectionery made me increasingly stressed.

One morning, on my way to work, I had a serious car accident. Another vehicle crashed into my door—the driver's seat was obliterated, but miraculously, I survived. With a concussion, a fractured pelvis, a compressed spine, and bruises all over, it took me four months to recover. I turned twenty during this time, though I didn't really celebrate—I was simply grateful to be alive.

Aware of the value of my life, I no longer wanted to work under such conditions. I didn't want to return to that job or that environment. I was eager to change paths and began exploring other professions and training opportunities.

Occupational therapy caught my attention, but after attending an information session, I realized it would require another three years of education. That didn't suit me. I didn't feel strong enough to return to studies or face the precariousness I had experienced during my apprenticeship. Moreover, my parents neither had the means nor the willingness to support me.

Still, the desire for change persisted. One day, while reading the newspaper, I came across an ad: "Confectioner wanted" at a chocolate factory in the region. I decided to give it a shot. This factory employed supervisors primarily to manage operations and workers, monitor production quality, and prepare praline fillings. The hours were much more manageable—with set start and finish times and weekends off. Of course, the work was very repetitive and left no room for the creativity I was accustomed to.

The person conducting the interview didn't understand why, with such excellent exam results and a passion for confectionery, I was applying for a factory job. He worried I might quickly become bored. When I explained my determination to change direction, he seemed to understand and decided to hire me.

I started on my twenty-first birthday. I was the first female confectioner at this company. My new supervisor gave me a tour of the various installations in the confectionery department. He introduced me to people we met along the way and left me in the capable hands of a confectioner colleague. This colleague took me through tunnels and hidden elevators to a small party in celebration of an employee's twenty years of service at the factory.

Although it was a cheerful event, it left a mark on me. While this colleague remained here doing the same thing day in and day out, I saw my entire life pass before me: my early childhood in Nods, the move to Landeron, my schooling, my apprenticeship, the start of my adult life. And all this time, he had been at this factory, moving pallets from one place to another. At that moment, I realized I didn't want to spend my entire life doing the same work!

I truly blossomed in this role. I had responsibilities, people trusted me, and I enjoyed the multicultural environment and the culinary specialties we shared during breaks.

I loved the giant machines dripping chocolate. I was sure each one had its own personality, becoming an entity of its own as it was surrounded by workers during the different production stages. My cheerful and sunny disposition helped me connect with and earn the appreciation of everyone. My role as a supervisor involved taking care of my production line, which included the machines and, more importantly, the people working on it. I listened to everyone. This approach was the answer to the question I later asked myself: How, at the age of twenty-one, did I gain the respect of team members who were often twice my age?

The factory operated under a management style we'd now call paternalistic. Personally, I liked being part of this big family, or even small village, given that there were over 500 employees. There was plenty of laughter around the installations, and I was fascinated by how we could spend an entire morning discussing chicken recipes.

A year after I started, the factory was bought by a German company. Restructuring followed, social benefits were reduced, and morale dropped. Less than a year later, it was sold again—this time to an American company. Production standards replaced quality, and the atmosphere changed drastically. I no longer felt aligned with the factory's values, which angered me as I felt neither my colleagues nor I were being respected.

During a vacation, I returned to the surprising news that my supervisor had temporarily reassigned me to the Research and Development (R&D) department to help develop a new chocolate bar. It was a dream role: flexible hours, interesting work, and a relaxed and friendly environment. Some colleagues had been there for 20, 30 years, or more. It seemed like the perfect job for the long term. My superior appreciated my work and requested my permanent transfer to R&D.

After a few years in this company, I realized I was too young to picture myself staying there until retirement. I started wondering what else I could do. I explored several ideas but found nothing concrete enough to take the leap.

One day, the idea of opening a crêperie came to me. It seemed like a small, enjoyable, and manageable project. This idea excited me and gave me the energy to take the necessary steps to move from idea to project. I needed a location, and one morning while reading the newspaper, I was astonished to find a crêperie for sale in Yverdon, a small town not far from home. I immediately went to see it.

Being an Aries, I didn't overthink things. It seemed obvious that this was the place, so I dove into the administrative steps and bank requirements. I also took time off to attend the mandatory restaurant management training course.

I moved to a village near my future business, and two months after celebrating my thirtieth birthday, I embarked on this new adventure.

Some time later, I heard on the radio that the factory I had left, along with the R&D department, was closing down and relocating to other production centers in Switzerland and Europe. The news sent chills up my spine—it was hard to imagine that this was the fate of the 175-year-old factory. Most employees lost their jobs, and the region lost part of its identity. I had left at the right time.

I poured my energy, time, and heart into my crêperie, giving the best of my creativity. The crêpe and galette menu evolved according to my inspirations, and the décor changed as I met different regional artists. I enjoyed implementing my ideas, transforming what seemed worth it, and creating a space that brought smiles, joyful breaks, and the possibility of healthy snacks and meals. Each new customer brought new energy; every interaction was a mirror that required clarity and grounding—a constant test.

I was also very proud to give the students working there well-deserved wages to help them partly finance their studies. The business grew more and more successful, often full at lunchtime, with evenings getting busier and busier, especially at weekends.

At thirty-six, I was diagnosed with HPV in my cervix. The infection wasn't advanced, and my gynecologist suggested I undergo a minor outpatient procedure involving an acid mixture to burn the infected area. However, my approach to healing is focused on addressing the root cause of "dis-ease." I therefore declined and instead requested biannual check-ups to monitor the progression of the infection.

A friend introduced me to Tantra training—a spiritual practice aimed at healing sexuality and resolving certain blockages. The training course was costly and time-consuming, but I reasoned that battling cancer would take more time and cost far more. In 2002, I began this journey, which opened me to a deeper self-awareness— energetically, spiritually, and physically—as well as to an alchemical integration of all aspects of being.

Alongside regular gynecological check-ups, after a year and a half, the infection regressed, and two years later, HPV was gone. Of course, I can't be sure whether my psychosomatic practices or other energy work cured me, but to me what mattered most was the result.

Once you experience personal development practices, it often opens a new path or vision. That was true for me. In parallel with running my crêperie, I trained in Reiki and a therapeutic method for navigating life's difficult transitions.

I also learned intuitive massage.

By then, most of my time was devoted to the crêperie—handling recurring problems, rush-hour service, and repetitive work. I began to feel stuck in a routine of crêpes. Stress-related allergies emerged. After 12 years, the project began weighing on me. I wanted to give myself the chance to pursue something new.

Some time later, I received a call from a man working in a business brokerage company. He told me someone was interested in buying my crêperie and had approached them for assistance. I was unsure—I had a great team around me, and the business was thriving. Curious about this unexpected opportunity, I agreed to a meeting. The potential buyer was genuinely interested; he had the financial means, loved the place, and wanted to keep it as a crêperie. He asked me to consider a price and make him an offer.

I didn't have any alternative projects in mind—just the vague idea of transitioning to a collective project. I had nothing solid to fall back on except the proceeds from the sale, which would give me time to adjust. Aware that if I didn't seize this opportunity, another might not come anytime soon, I agreed to the sale. I came up with a fair price, which was accepted. The buyer and the brokerage company handled all the paperwork, and two months later, I handed over the keys and bid farewell to the people and the place.

Now, I had to find my footing again. Confident that life would present me with something new, I stayed attentive to my heart, my desires. Two aspirations emerged: improving my English and spending time in the Findhorn community in Scotland. On the community's website, I found a program offering "English and community living." A chance to fulfill both dreams simultaneously! I registered for the next session.

In the meantime, my mother passed away. She was only sixty-five but had been ill for as long as I could remember. She had miraculously survived several serious illnesses and I had thought of her as immortal. I was grateful to have the time to mourn her and say goodbye without needing to rearrange my life to make time.

At Findhorn, the entire English class was made up of people transitioning in life—career changes, new directions, reorientations. I hadn't realized the community was such a transformative place. Residents of the community had even created a personal development tool called the "Transformation Game." They liked to say that the community's god was compost. At the community's inception, the three founders had cultivated vegetables on sandy soil enriched with compost they created themselves, nurturing their plants with presence and energy. Their legendary harvests were stunning.

Upon my return, I wanted "intelligent" holidays. A Swiss friend involved in a children's home project in India invited me to join, and I spent two months volunteering. These were certainly not holidays in the traditional sense. Humanitarian work still raises many questions for me today.

The next phase came with a proposal to create a venue for workshops, celebrations, and retreats. I thought, "Here's my collective project, the new door I was waiting for." The proposed location was a small château once occupied by a community of artists. For a year, I dedicated my time to clearing and renovating the house's interior to prepare it for guests.

During this year, my father passed away. It was all becoming too much. No stable professional activity to rely on, no mother, no apartment, and now no father. I felt like a balloon floating in the air with nothing to anchor me down.

Even the workshop house project began to feel increasingly utopian. Everyone wanted to pursue their own dreams, pulling in different directions, and the shared goal became a pretext. Feeling caught in the middle, I brought it up in a meeting. They didn't understand my concerns and assured me otherwise. Far from reassured, I left the project. Not long after its official launch, disagreements among the members escalated, and it ended in court.

I reflected on my massage training and the dance workshops I had been leading for years. I realized my professional future likely lay in this direction—a solo project again, at least for now.

I resumed training, focusing on certifications that would later allow me to offer reimbursement through complementary health insurance for consultations in natural medicine. These professional courses were expensive and time-consuming, requiring significant individual work alongside the lessons. Living with very little, my world grew smaller, and I found myself back in a mindset of scarcity, a reality that I created for myself.

During this period, I took on small jobs to "make ends meet," at one point juggling up to five roles, including building my new massage clientele.

After some time, I was able to dedicate myself entirely to massage therapy. Today, my financial resources come solely from this work, and I have been established in Le Landeron as a massage therapist for ten years. I am grateful for the flow of my journey, the courage to listen to my needs, and the ability to embrace the small and large miracles of life.

A new turn is beginning now, still in therapeutic massage but with a more holistic approach. I feel drawn to something more connected—not just to the entirety of being but also in vibrational alignment with the evolution of the whole.

I don't know if this kind of care exists yet. I already have glimpses of it and look forward to discovering what's next.

SYNCHRONICITIES AND OPPORTUNITIES

Governed by the laws of the quantum system, synchronicities and opportunities are part of this vast network of individual and collective creations, formed by the vibrations of thoughts, needs, desires, fears, beliefs, and much more from living beings.

Many books have been written on this topic, including *Managing Thought, Attracting Abundance in All Its Forms, The Power of Intention*, and countless works on coaching—a field that has seen remarkable growth in recent years.

Personally, I have experienced these coincidences, these answered prayers, in my life. Naturally, I became interested in the creative power of thought. I read books, attended various workshops, watched videos, and carefully crafted requests and mantras intended to make my life more beautiful—even perfect.

For me, gratitude is one of the primary keys, if not the primary key, that provides us with the energy and vibration needed to connect to this network. Gratitude helps me accept what is and prevents me from feeling like a victim, because most of the time, I have created or subconsciously chosen to experience the situation. Gratitude brings me joy, enthusiasm, and a sense of wonder.

One beautiful synchronicity related to the gratitude I was exploring at the time manifested into the form of a gift: the *Gratitude Stone* by Eileen Caddy, one of the founders of the Findhorn community.

I am grateful that I am able to recognize when a situation doesn't suit me. Acknowledging this awareness gives me the impulse for change. This shift in energy sets the network of abundance in motion or accelerates it.

Synchronicities and opportunities aligned with my new energy manifest in various forms to bring solutions, answers, a new vision, and—most importantly—a reconnection to my "essence of life." I've observed that when I am on vacation, lightheartedly living in the present moment, synchronicities abound and effortlessly guide me toward what is perfect for me. If I face a challenge, someone often appears at just the right time to offer help. I've frequently been amazed by the presence of these people at precisely the right moment.

Being in the present moment, immersed in joy, gratitude, enthusiasm, and wonder—with the lightheartedness of a child—elevates me to a vibration that attracts the best for me in that moment and fulfills my needs.

I've made the choice to live in the present moment. For me, rather than creating imaginary needs and believing that my happiness depends on their fulfillment, I find it far more pleasant to be joyful about what I'm experiencing in the here and now.

Richard Phan

HOW SILICON VALLEY TRANSFORMED ME INTO AN ENTREPRENEUR

Richard Phan is an entrepreneur passionate about technological innovation.

With parents who left Vietnam in the 1950s, Richard was born in Paris. He earned his engineering degree and worked in Paris before moving to Grenoble to join Hewlett-Packard. The following year, Richard and his family relocated to Santa Clara, California. During his seven years in Silicon Valley, Richard worked in Cupertino, Mountain View, and Sunnyvale for Hewlett-Packard, Handspring, and Palm Computing. Upon returning to France in 2004, Richard and his family settled in Annecy.

An entrepreneur since 2011, Richard is now a member, elected administrator, and board member of the *Réseau Entreprendre Haute-Savoie*. This association supports business leaders in launching or acquiring enterprises. Richard has also volunteered with *100,000 Entrepreneurs* (an organization dedicated to instilling the spirit and desire to pursue entrepreneurship in young people aged 13 to 25) and *60,000 Rebonds* (an organization that helps entrepreneurs who have liquidated their businesses transition to new professional projects).

Today, Richard is based in Lyon and continues to focus on innovation, product development, CO2 capture, and Artificial Intelligence.

LinkedIn: https://linkedin.com/in/richardphan

Richard Phan

HOW SILICON VALLEY TRANSFORMED ME INTO AN ENTREPRENEUR

The people who are crazy enough to think they can change the world are the ones who do.

—Steve Jobs

I had the privilege of living and working for seven years in the heart of Silicon Valley, precisely at the time when Google and Facebook were emerging. Having arrived at the dawn of the golden age of internet, I also experienced the economic downturn known as the "dot-com bubble burst."

This cultural immersion was rich and full of lessons across so many domains. I will share with you how this environment profoundly changed me, compelling me to question myself and evolve in self-confidence and my vision of leadership.

MY JOURNEY WEST

I arrived in California the month I turned 28, and was a product of French republican meritocracy. The son of Vietnamese parents who arrived in France with almost nothing, I rigorously and diligently pursued my studies. I was strong in math and had obtained a scholarship. Encouraged by my mother (thank you, Mom), I passed the entrance exam to a prestigious computer engineering school. Before arriving in Santa Clara, I had had early professional experiences at a small company in Paris, followed by Hewlett-Packard (HP) in Grenoble in 1996. The following year, HP transferred me to Silicon Valley.

In 1997, Netscape, the very first mainstream web browser, was released. The predecessor of today's Edge, Chrome, and Firefox, it allowed millions to easily browse the internet and introduced the concept of hyperlinks for seamless navigation between sites. Google was born a year later, in 1998, and soon displaced all other search engines now long forgotten: Altavista, Inktomi, Yahoo…

In this digital gold rush, I was an engineer at HP, the first start-up of Silicon Valley according to local legend, which had since grown into a multinational. The company's founders started in their garage and sold their first product to Disney, which used it for the Fantasia soundtrack. In 1997, HP was known as an engineering-first company, creating highly specialized, reliable products for an audience of engineers. Marketing at HP was so secondary that it was said if HP made sushi, they would market it as "dead, raw, cold fish." HP was also famous for its forward-thinking, humanistic company culture, the HP Way, which showed deep respect for its employees. Layoffs, though easy in the United States, were considered a last resort. Employees who underperformed were given a second chance, and "being made redundant" was not part of the culture. Internal mobility was encouraged, and the closure of a business unit rarely meant job loss.

Despite this comfortable and reassuring environment for foreign employees, I felt the need for a change. Nothing is ever perfect, and "politics" had developed at HP—the art of advancing careers through appearances and personal alliances rather than talent and achievements. As one manager put it, it's like beer: there's the foam, and then underneath there's the beer. At HP, I found there was too much foam, and I'd had enough.

In 2001, I joined a highly promising start-up, Handspring. Now mostly forgotten, this start-up had the highest growth rate at the time. Founded in 1998 by the original creators of Palm (do you remember Palm Pilots?), it raised nearly $250 million immediately due to the founders' reputation and their vision of a handheld, wireless-connected device—at a time when Wi-Fi was barely emerging, and 2G was not yet fully deployed. A year later, their first product (without Wi-Fi or 2G) was already in stores across the United States and soon around the world. Another year later, in May 2000, just two years after its creation, Handspring went public on NASDAQ and raised another $200 million.

The dot-com bubble burst began in March 2000. Thus, I joined Handspring the following year, amidst economic turmoil. My future manager, noting my French background, repeatedly emphasized that my employment contract was "at will," meaning the company made no guarantees about the stability of my position, which could be terminated without justification. I assured him I understood what "at will" meant. But had I really grasped its implications?

SHOCK AND FEAR

It was within this context that the burst of the dot-com bubble, initially a stock market phenomenon, began to trigger an economic crisis for companies in the digital technology sector. Although our work was not directly related to developing public internet, our sales plummeted, as did those of our main competitor, Palm. Having never achieved profitability, Handspring was drawing from its financial reserves, which were rapidly dwindling. Now a publicly traded company, it had to release its financial results quarterly, along with forecasts for the upcoming quarter.

The first wave of layoffs at Handspring caused an enormous shock wave among employees. More than 10% of the workforce was affected. Even when handled humanely, it remains a harsh announcement. The information had to stay confidential as long as possible, as it could impact the stock price. It was typically shared publicly during the quarterly earnings announcement, after which affected employees met with human resources for a highly scripted conversation—prepared in such a way as to prevent potential legal claims, especially for discrimination. Legally, the notice period for layoffs in the U.S. was two weeks, but in practice, no one stayed for that duration. This meant that terminated employees left the same day with their personal belongings and a check for half a month's salary.

This is where the generosity of European unemployment insurance systems becomes apparent. At that time in California, unemployment coverage lasted a maximum of six months, with compensation capped at around $1,600 per month (in 2001), regardless of previous salary. In Silicon Valley, this amount barely covered the rent for a modest two-bedroom apartment. Health insurance, fully employer-funded, also became an additional burden for the ex-employee—a significant one, given the exorbitant healthcare costs in the U.S. For a family of expatriates, where often only one spouse worked and there were one or more dependent children, the question of returning home arose quickly if no new job was secured immediately.

I found myself at the forefront of a situation I had not anticipated: an employee at a struggling company, with an "at will" contract, a non-working wife, and two children aged 2 and 4. I could lose my job at any quarter, with no guarantee of finding another, amidst an economic crisis that forced companies to lay off rather than hire. Horror stories—anecdotes, perhaps exaggerated but illustrating how quickly the fortune of Silicon Valley engineers could reverse—began to circulate. Common were tales of families spending their last dollars on plane tickets to move in with their parents in Europe, rumors of credit-financed Porsches abandoned on the way to the airport, and news stories about engineers becoming homeless in San Francisco within just a few months.

Not being part of the first wave of layoffs felt like I had miraculously dodged a devastating cannonball. It was a warning. Having started my career in France under the protective status of permanent contracts and after more than three years at Hewlett-Packard, which rarely laid off employees and offered additional severance, I now felt at the mercy of fate, with severe consequences for my family if it happened. I was afraid.

I had never been so afraid. Being financially responsible for my family's well-being and facing the possibility of losing that security overnight was daunting. What to do?

SELF-CONFIDENCE

At first, this fear paralyzed me. Then, I analyzed the situation as coldly and objectively as possible. On one hand, I noted that while some employees had to leave each quarter, the vast majority stayed. On the other hand, I observed that those who found new jobs quickly did so thanks to their network and reputation. It is no coincidence that LinkedIn appeared around this time (2003), as it digitized the networking practices of Silicon Valley.

The question, therefore, was not "What will I do if I lose my job?" but rather "How can I make sure I never lose it?" This shift in mindset is profound. Instead of being passively subjected to an event, one assumes an active posture with a clear objective. This approach implies two fundamental concepts: first, the belief that one can influence the course of events through actions and decisions, and second, and most importantly, self-confidence in one's skills and abilities.

The first answer to this new question was, "I will never be on a list of employees at risk of being laid off." To ensure I would never be on this dangerous list, the most effective approach in this pragmatic and minimally political company was to perform as well as possible in the tasks assigned to me. Not only to be the best I could be, but to excel in a field that could be easily quantified in dollars. If what I brought to the company in terms of revenue or cost savings significantly exceeded my salary, there would be no reason for the company to let me go.

I immediately applied this strategy: identify the most beneficial projects for the team and the company, commit fully, and deliver undeniable and measurable results (preferably in dollars). Another advantage of this approach was that it noticeably enhanced my reputation. This reputation served as a safeguard in case of job loss: with an excellent reputation among my colleagues, I would be able to find a new job more quickly elsewhere.

Ultimately, this fear proved very beneficial for the rest of my career. By applying this healthy strategy that aligned with my personality, I was never on a list of employees at risk and progressed within this remarkable start-up. I faced this fear by confronting it, tackling the sources of potential job loss, and drawing from my internal resources. I had confidence in myself, and this confidence only grew stronger. I never feared losing my job again.

WHAT IS LEADERSHIP?

Another one of my experiences at Handspring helped me understand what is meant by leadership, a word that doesn't translate well into French. Could it be described as "the ability to lead a team"? On this topic, it is very instructive to compare the job description for a Project Manager on the job search site Indeed, in both its English and French versions.

On Indeed.com, the page "8 qualities of an effective project manager" lists "Leadership skills, Communication skills, Problem-solving skills" as the top qualities. Under the Leadership section, it reads: "Being a good leader means that you can motivate your team to perform at their best throughout the project and ensure all team members have a clear understanding of what is expected of them."

On Indeed.fr, the page "Quelles sont les qualités d'un chef de projet ?" (What are the Qualities of a Project Manager) lists "Organizational skills, attention to detail, ability to delegate" as the primary qualities and "Initiative" as the last. However, it does not mention team motivation or the importance of clear communication of each team member's responsibilities.

This cultural difference is worth considering!

Within the previously mentioned turbulent context, Handspring appointed me to a position I had never held before: Manufacturing Program Manager. My role was to manage the project for industrializing an electronic product. The R&D department had designed the product, and our industrialization team was responsible for ensuring it could be manufactured in large quantities. This task was managed as a project under my leadership.

An important stage in an industrialization project is to produce prototypes on the production line that will be used for mass production. This allows the product design to be tested in a real production environment, complete with its challenges, operators, tools, and adjustments, and to re-adjust the design to facilitate production and improve quality.

The entire industrialization team, therefore, traveled to the production site, where we arrived early in the morning. The dozen Handspring members enthusiastically met with our subcontractor's production team. Conversations were lively, and the project team distributed themselves across the production line.

I was myself engaged in a spontaneous conversation with my local counterpart.

And almost suddenly, toward the end of the morning, I lifted my head and realized that, in fact, no one had actually started working—that is, engaging in concrete tasks that would lead to the production of these prototypes. Initially surprised, I immediately wondered why.

Then reality hit me square in the face: it was because I, the Program Manager, had not told my team what I expected from the day, nor had I checked with them to ensure they understood what needed to be done individually and collectively. They continued calmly chatting because I wasn't doing my job as a leader! In reality, they were all waiting for me to do my job!

As soon as I realized this, I called my colleagues together for an impromptu meeting. Together all standing in front of a whiteboard, we outlined the day's goal, the intermediate steps, the necessary tasks, and their sequence. Everyone could contribute, enhance the plan, ask questions—my role was to create this moment, provide the general objective of the day, and arbitrate if necessary between conflicting priorities.

As I mentioned, my colleagues were exceptionally skilled, and it didn't take long for the plan to be written on the whiteboard, agreed upon by all, and for them to get to work immediately.

I slipped into this leadership role almost instantaneously. It gave me a new and immense sense of professional satisfaction. I loved having this central role as a guide, decision-maker, and team leader. It was a source of pride to be useful, necessary to this team effort, and to be accepted as such by colleagues whose technical expertise I greatly admired. It was also a responsibility—a "pressure," as one might say in French—to lead the team in the chosen direction and make the right decisions along the way. It is important to note that my colleagues' professionalism and kindness greatly helped me in my accelerated learning of what a leadership role is.

SELF-CONFIDENCE + LEADERSHIP = ?

These two moments, which likely went unnoticed by even my close circle, triggered profound changes in the way I thought and acted professionally.

I am convinced that my entrepreneurial life, which began several years later, has its roots precisely in these two moments. Starting out requires strong self-confidence and a desire to take on a leadership role. Unfortunately, these are two qualities that are neither highlighted nor even encouraged in our educational and social systems. On the contrary, these traits are often criticized and viewed as arrogance.

Ultimately, it was staying for an extended period in a different environment—Silicon Valley—that allowed me to experience and understand these cultural aspects that were so different from those I had previously known. It's not a question of judging one culture superior to another. It's about going beyond superficial criticism, biased by our prejudices and cultural background, to truly understand the logic and reasoning of those who speak a different language. This can only enrich us and allow us to take what we appreciate most from each culture.

SYNCHRONICITY OR SERENDIPITY

These experiences changed me, but they very well might not have. How do we recognize the potential of these moments and pause to learn from them and change?

It all starts with acknowledging an abnormal state—an unexpected, intense negative emotion (in my case, the fear of losing my job), an unusual, unforeseen situation (no one working). Then, knowing how to step back, avoid automatic reactions, and begin by humbly questioning oneself: What if the anomaly was because of me, my actions, or my lack of decision-making? Humility is not contradictory to self-confidence; on the contrary, having self-confidence does not mean believing oneself to be perfect. It means recognizing one's weaknesses and knowing how to draw on strengths and skills to continue learning and building one's life path to become even better.

Embrace contact with other cultures, take on challenges, and learn about others and yourself! Living within communities that have different cultures and histories helps us better understand our own. You don't need to go far; ways of thinking and living are already very different in Germany, Italy, Switzerland, or Spain. This immersion allows us to put isolated anecdotes we hear into a global context and prevents us from dismissing them too quickly, as we tend to compare them to our social and cultural references. By understanding the logic, culture, and way of thinking of our neighbors, we will live in better harmony with them and succeed in building great things together. And sometimes, different ways of thinking will provoke profound changes in our way of being.

Jasmyne L. Langlois

MY LIFE SYNCHRONICITIES

Born on February 4, 1989, Jasmyne L. Langlois is a rising figure in the Quebec artistic scene, combining expertise in management with a passion for the arts.

From a young age, she was drawn to visual arts, an interest that led her to explore various creative fields, including drawing, dance, and pottery.

Her professional journey began in the field of management before she joined a major art gallery in Quebec, where she honed her skills in cultural management. During her studies, she worked in insurance while actively participating in student associations, which helped her develop a strong ability to juggle multiple responsibilities.

Today, Jasmyne is the proud owner of her own gallery, *Espace Langlois*, located in Old Montreal. She represents both renowned artists and emerging talents. Her gallery has become a must-visit space for art enthusiasts and stands as one of her most remarkable achievements. At the same time, she is pursuing a certificate in art history, furthering her expertise in the field and fueling her future ambitions.

Guided by her core values—following her instincts and spreading positivity—Jasmyne aims to go even further. Among her goals, she envisions giving lectures and contributing to redefining the history of art through her actions and future projects.

Gallery website: www.espacelanglois.com

Gallery Instagram: *espacelanglois*

Personal Instagram: *llangloisj*

Gallery Facebook: *Espace Langlois*

Jasmyne L. Langlois

MY LIFE SYNCHRONICITIES

When we want something, all the Universe conspires
in helping us to achieve it.

– Paulo Coelho

A PASSION FOR ART FROM A YOUNG AGE

Art has always been an obvious path for me, a kind of refuge where I could lose and find myself at the same time. In school, whenever given a choice, I instinctively gravitated toward art classes, whether it was art history or visual arts. For me, it wasn't just a school activity; it was a visceral passion, a way of exploring the world and understanding myself.

CROSSROADS

Around the age of 14, two conversations with my father marked a turning point in my life. These serious discussions left a weight I will never forget. The first was about the dangers of cannabis, a topic I'll quickly move past. The second concerned my future and left an indelible mark on my journey.

My father, whose wisdom was tinged with pragmatism, painted the image of an artistic career in a somewhat harsh light. He wasn't trying to discourage me but rather to prepare me for a life filled with uncertainties, sacrifices, and perhaps even disillusionment. His advice, which I followed, was to keep art as a passion while studying something more "concrete," something that would open more doors.

THE 'BUSINESS' PATH

This is why I chose to study business, a path that seemed safer. After my management studies, I secured an internship in the hospitality sector. I had accepted it thinking it would be an entry point into a stable and fulfilling career, and it was, but I hadn't considered the working conditions. As a manager, I had the heavy burden of supervising employees, most of whom had been working in the company since its inception. Their experience should have been a source of inspiration, but I quickly realized that their longevity came with a cynicism that was difficult to manage. As for the clients they too could be unpleasant, sometimes engaging in unclean behavior, such as spitting on the ground to ward off bad luck, out of superstition.

Day by day, I felt increasingly more like a stranger in this environment. I realized that my future did not lie there, in these constraining hours, in these repetitive tasks that left no room for creativity.

Thanks to this internship, I understood that I didn't want this life or to lose myself in a career that didn't resonate with me. I realized that stability isn't the only thing that matters. It was time to truly look within, to seek what I genuinely desired for my future.

A NEW PATH OPENS

After this realization, I gave myself time to reflect, to understand what my driving force was truly. I wanted a job where every day would feel like an adventure, in a place where people would come to work out of passion not obligation. I had traveled in Australia for 18 months before starting university, a period during which I felt freer and more alive than ever. I understood that this freedom was what I sought above all.

My choice naturally turned to the Old Port of Montreal, a neighborhood rich in culture, history, and life. Armed with determination, I walked the streets with my resume in hand, ready to hand it out in person but to my surprise, no one wanted a paper resume – I was already out of sync with the modern job market.

As I wandered aimlessly, I stumbled upon an art gallery. Behind the glass, one artwork particularly drew me in: two enormous eyes seemed to be staring at me, as if probing my soul. I felt that something special was happening here. Driven by an impulse I couldn't ignore, I walked in. At the front desk, I asked a question that would change the course of my life: "What does it take to work here?" The response was direct: "You need to be good at sales."

I knew I had that skill. That evening, in my small studio apartment, I searched the internet, found a job listing, and applied. Two months later, as my birthday approached, I received the long-awaited call: I was hired.

A NEW BEGINNING

I will never forget my first days at the gallery. From the moment I walked through the door as an employee, I knew I had found my place. The staff welcomed me warmly. I met colleagues who, though I didn't know it yet, would become close friends and everyday companions.

One day, during my training period, we gathered in the back room for lunch. They shared their journeys and experiences with me, and something in me opened up. The emotions I had been holding back overwhelmed me, and I started to cry, but these weren't tears of sadness. I felt a deep relief, the intense feeling of finally having found what I had been searching for for so many years: a place where I felt at home.

IN SEARCH OF LIFE'S ESSENCE

After finding my place in the art world, I felt the need to escape again, to plunge into an adventure that would bring me even closer to myself. I decided to spend a month in Thailand, a journey with no set itinerary, guided by my instinct and desire for freedom.

I had only booked the first four days in Bangkok. The rest of my trip, I intended to improvise as I went along, following the flow of encounters and discoveries. For two weeks, I lost myself in this fascinating country, far from everything I knew. Each day was a new exploration, another step toward the unknown.

Then some day, as I wandered aimlessly, I heard a voice in the distance: "You want some macaroni salad?" in a distinctly Québécois accent. It had been two weeks since I had encountered anyone from my home country. You can imagine the warmth it brought to my heart. Intrigued, I turned around and saw Vanessa, an expat I would soon get to know. We exchanged a few words, and she invited me to join her at her "shop." I quickly fell in love with the island she had moved to a few years earlier: Koh Tao. I stayed there for two weeks, sharing many drinks and coffees with her, our feet in the crystalline turquoise water. This serendipitous meeting marked the beginning of a deep friendship.

Vanessa and I crossed paths many times around the world, exchanging profound reflections on life, freedom, happiness, and spirituality.

A NEW LOVE

When I returned home, I felt different, more in tune with myself. Then COVID turned our lives upside down, and Vanessa decided to sell her business and spend the summer in Montreal. She quarantined at my place.

It was during this time that I met Daniel, who would become my partner. Meanwhile, Vanessa met a Swiss man and embarked on a new adventure in his home country.

THE REALIZATION OF A DREAM

After Daniel and I moved in together, an idea began to take root, almost naturally, as the pandemic dragged on. Since I was young, I had harbored a deep desire to start my own entrepreneurial project, an ambition that felt like a natural part of me. At first, I thought it might be a restaurant, then I considered a café, and now that I was working in a gallery, I realized it was a type of business I truly loved. I often talked to Daniel about it, sharing my childhood dreams with him.

Daniel, who worked as an assistant to Louis Boudreault, a well-known Québécois artist with both local and international recognition, started discussing the idea with him. Louis, always ready to encourage new initiatives, casually told Daniel that if the idea came to fruition, it would be possible to exhibit his works on our walls. I still remember the moment—we were having lunch when Daniel shared this conversation with me. As soon as he uttered the words, telling me Louis was willing to have his works displayed, a sense of certainty overwhelmed me: this was the opportunity I had been waiting for all my life. Without a moment's hesitation, I seized it.

Looking back now, I realize it was the perfect alignment of the stars. From that moment, everything fell into place. I prepared a budget and began searching for a space. Two weeks later, I found it. The name, the logo, the artists whom Daniel was helping me contact—it all started coming together. I knew exactly what was needed: good lighting, a reliable payment system, and an effective hanging system. Miraculously, everything seemed to align perfectly, as if the universe were conspiring in our favor.

SUPPORT IN SWITZERLAND

Meanwhile, Vanessa, now living in Switzerland with her new partner, wanted to start a business as well. She asked for my help, and I took the opportunity to step back from my job. I resigned from the art gallery and went to visit her. It was a rejuvenating break, a moment to catch my breath before everything truly took off in Quebec.

THE LAUNCH

Upon my return, everything accelerated. Daniel and I officially launched our project. He was an immense source of support, especially during the first steps of this adventure. Thanks to my work experience and studies in business, I had a clear vision of the gallery's needs. Everything seemed to flow naturally, as if every step of my past had prepared me for this moment. The path leading to the gallery's opening was so smooth, so synchronized! It felt like a gift from above.

In no time at all, we opened the gallery's doors, and the first year was a great success. Today, Daniel is no longer part of the team. Times have changed, and the art market is going through a challenging period but that's part of an entrepreneur's journey—you have to be able to adapt to any situation. It has now been three years since I opened the gallery in the Old Port of Montreal.

THE ART OF PATIENCE AND SYNCHRONICITY

Taking the time to reflect on all this makes me realize just how rich my journey has been in terms of growth. I've had to die and be reborn countless times to rise to the challenges that came my way. I had to grieve my relationship with Daniel while continuing to work with him and eventually came to want the gallery for myself alone. Speaking of grief, I've had to acknowledge and accept all the limits of my being. I had to come to terms with the fact that having a gallery wasn't quite what I had expected.

I endured periods of stagnation that felt endless, as though I were stuck in one place forever because I didn't know how to move forward. Some moments of solitude were so long and so deep that they hurt. I wanted things to happen, and I wanted them to happen immediately. I wanted everyone to know about the gallery. I wanted to change the history of art. I put so much pressure on my shoulders that it paralyzed me and made me sick, pushing me to the brink of burnout.

Too often, I forget that patience and perseverance are essential keys to overcoming any challenge, as life follows an order we don't always understand.

The moments when nothing seemed to be happening were always the most frightening. These periods of emptiness, of uncertainty, were when doubt crept in, when I questioned everything. Yet, looking back, I realize these moments of apparent calm were never meaningless. They functioned like waves, receding to return stronger, making way for new movements and new connections.

These periods have, in fact, been crucial moments of death and rebirth for me. They exist to prepare the ground, to allow things to align before the next step, before the next surge of growth. As I write these lines, I've come to see that they are an integral part of the transformation process, where everything converges to guide us toward unexpected synchronicities.

Ultimately, life is a school of patience. Every moment, every silence, every doubt is an opportunity to let your roots grow deeper, to let realignments take place. I must learn to be at peace with these periods of stillness, to understand that they are part of my path, preparing for every new stage of my inner growth and every moment of perfect synchronicity.

Gyambo Nb

MY JOURNEY TOWARD A ZERO-WASTE BHUTAN

Gyambo Nb is a citizen of the small country of Bhutan where he was born and has lived his entire life. Bhutan is heralded around the world for its commitment to fostering gross national happiness (GNH).

Gyambo works as a guide who accompanies groups on tours of his beautiful Bhutan. In his spare time, Gyambo is a committed champion of solid waste management, Gyambo regularly goes on garbage-collecting walks in Bhutan villages and the countryside to help keep his country clean.

Follow Gyambo on:
Facebook: gyambo.nb.1
LinkedIn: gyambo-nb

Gyambo Nb

MY JOURNEY TOWARD A ZERO-WASTE BHUTAN

To Their Majesties King Jigme Singye Wangchuck, the architect of the philosophy of Gross National Happiness, and Queen Jetsun Pema Wangchuck, for whom 'the preservation of our environment is essential for our survival and happiness.'

INTRODUCTION

I hail from Nabji, a remote village in Korphu Gewog, located in the Trongsa Dzongkhag of Bhutan. This village is not just my home; it is steeped in historical significance. According to our traditions, it is believed that Guru Rinpoche, the second Buddha, entered Bhutan through Nabji in 847 AD, which makes this place not only a geographical location but a spiritual gateway that connects our rich cultural heritage to the natural world around us.

Growing up in such a historical and spiritual context has shaped my understanding of the environment and the responsibility we bear to protect it. My educational journey began at the tender age of five, and it was quite a challenge to reach school. I had to walk for three days just to get to the nearest motor road, followed by a two-hour truck ride to reach my hometown, Trongsa. This journey often involved spending nights in the forest, in small villages, or alongside the motorway, all of which instilled in me a profound appreciation for the land and its offerings.

I attended Trongsa Shcrabling Junior High School, which provided an English-medium education for ten years. Following that, I continued my studies at Zhemgang High School and Jakar High School before moving to Kalimpong, India. After completing my education, I returned to Bhutan and worked as a salesperson in a video cassette shop. Eventually, I bought the shop and ran it for several years. However, in 1999, I felt a calling to become a guide and underwent training, this marking the beginning of a new chapter in my life.

THE ROLE OF A TOUR GUIDE

As a tour guide, I have had the privilege of interacting with many guests from around the world. One common remark that I have consistently received is, "Wow! Your country is clean and beautiful. We can breathe fresh air here." This feedback was a source of pride for me, as it reflected the collective efforts of my fellow Bhutanese to maintain the beauty of our homeland. However, I also recognized a growing concern regarding waste, especially with the increase in tourism.

The issue of waste became increasingly apparent to me as I guided tourists through our breathtaking landscapes. While visitors often marveled at Bhutan's pristine environment, the reality of littering and waste accumulation was a stark contrast to the admiration they expressed. I realized that I needed to do something meaningful to protect our environment, not only for the present but also for future generations. Inspired by our Queen's initiative to achieve zero waste by 2030, I felt compelled to take action. I wanted to showcase Bhutan's rich culture and maintain a clean environment while doing so.

BUDDHIST BELIEFS AND ENVIRONMENTAL STEWARDSHIP

As a Buddhist, I hold a profound belief in the interconnectedness of all living beings. We believe that every stream, river, tree, and mountain has life and an owner—often a local deity who protects these elements. Neglecting our environment not only disrespects these deities but also threatens our well-being. We have seen the emergence of new diseases linked to environmental degradation, and I understood that it was my responsibility to take action.

In Bhutan, we view waste as something detrimental—not just to our physical surroundings, but to our spiritual health as well. The accumulation of waste can be seen as an evil that disrupts the harmony of nature. This belief system deeply influences my approach to environmental advocacy. I felt a calling to educate my fellow

Bhutanese and tourists about the importance of preserving our environment and minimizing waste.

A PERSONAL ENCOUNTER THAT SPARKED MY MISSION

My journey toward environmental advocacy truly began in 1999 when I welcomed a group of Canadian guests at Paro International Airport, our only international airport. Upon landing, they expressed their apprehension due to the rocky landing conditions. However, as soon as they settled into the car, their first words were about the beauty and cleanliness of Bhutan. They marveled at the fresh air and the pristine landscapes, expressing their admiration for our environment. Their appreciation ignited a spark within me—a desire to ensure that Bhutan remains as pristine as they experienced it.

One day, while hiking with guests to the Tiger's Nest Monastery, I noticed litter left behind by other hikers—packaging from lunch boxes and plastic water bottles. It was embarrassing to see this waste in such a revered location. In that moment, I realized that I could not ignore the trash surrounding me. I picked up the litter and carried it in my backpack, committing to clean up whenever I hiked. This small act of picking up trash during my hikes became a significant turning point in my life.

FACING CHALLENGES AND OVERCOMING DOUBTS

Initially, my fellow guides teased me, suggesting that I was only doing it for better tips from the guests. They didn't understand my motivations and laughed at my efforts to maintain cleanliness. To avoid their ridicule, I had to hide my cleaning activities, discreetly filling my bag during hikes. However, on June 26, 2019, everything changed. I saw our Queen and one of the head monks on BBS (Bhutan Broadcasting Service) participating in a cleanup campaign. This public display of commitment to cleanliness inspired me to make a promise to myself: I would engage in cleaning activities every week, specifically on Saturdays, and on significant occasions in our country.

After this realization, I began to dedicate myself to cleaning efforts with renewed vigor. I organized local cleanup campaigns, gathering friends and community members to join me. Each Saturday, we would venture into the mountains or the valleys to pick up litter, demonstrating our commitment to protecting our environment. Through these efforts, I also aimed to raise awareness among my fellow Bhutanese about the importance of keeping our land clean.

MY CLEANING CAMPAIGNS AND COMMUNITY INVOLVEMENT

In 2022, I incorporated a "Zero Waste Hour" into my routine, a concept introduced by our Queen, who is also the patron of the environment. This initiative resonated deeply within me as I sought to engage more community members in the fight against waste. However, just as my efforts began to take shape, the COVID-19 pandemic disrupted my cleaning activities, halting tourism and my campaigns. The lockdown was a challenging time for many, including myself, as I missed my cleaning routine; it had become an integral part of my life.

The pandemic highlighted the fragility of our systems, and it also demonstrated the necessity of community solidarity. Our King's response to the pandemic was inspiring; he established the Druk Gyalpo's Relief Kidu Office, providing essential support, including food and medicine, to those affected. Witnessing his dedication to the well-being of our people motivated me to give back. I decided to organize a cleaning campaign in honor of our King's birthday, advocating for cleanliness along national highways.

On February 21, 2021, I drove to Paro Drukgyal Dzong, offering prayers for our King's health and committed to cleaning the national highway. With the help of friends and children, I set out on my mission, collecting a Bolero pickup truck full of garbage along the way. This campaign was not just about cleaning; it was a way to express gratitude for the support our King had given to the tourism sector during the pandemic.

Despite the challenges of the pandemic, I remained determined to continue my advocacy work. I organized smaller community cleanups, ensuring that safety measures were in place. Each cleaning event allowed me to pray for our King and Queen and express my gratitude for their leadership and vision for a cleaner Bhutan.

On June 4th, 2022, coinciding with our Queen's birthday, I embarked on a remarkable journey across Bhutan. Over the span of ninety-four days, I walked the country, advocating for environmental cleanliness, clearing litter and raising awareness. During this journey, twenty-two Dzongs and twenty-eight cremation grounds were cleaned.

KEY LOCATIONS IN MY JOURNEY

Throughout my campaigns, I have worked in several significant locations that hold cultural and spiritual importance in Bhutan. Each place has its unique challenges and rewards, and the communities in these areas have played a crucial role in supporting my efforts.

1. Paro Valley: Known for its stunning landscapes and the iconic Tiger's Nest Monastery, Paro Valley is a significant area for tourism in Bhutan. My cleaning campaigns here often attract local volunteers, including students from nearby schools. Their enthusiasm inspires me and reinforces the idea that the younger generation is eager to protect our environment. Engaging with the local community has allowed us to foster a sense of shared responsibility for keeping our surroundings clean.

2. Thimphu: The capital city, Thimphu, is where I have engaged with various organizations and government bodies to promote environmental awareness. Collaborating with local NGOs has allowed me to expand my reach and involve more people in waste management initiatives. The support from community leaders has been instrumental in driving our campaigns forward.

3. Bumthang: This region is known for its religious significance, with numerous monasteries and temples. While cleaning in Bumthang, I was able to connect with the local monks, who are pivotal in educating their communities about environmental stewardship. Their support has been invaluable, as they encourage their followers to respect nature and minimize waste.

4. Wangdue Phodrang: This district is rich in natural beauty and biodiversity. While organizing cleanup drives here, I have had the opportunity to engage with local farmers and business owners, discussing sustainable practices and waste reduction strategies that can benefit both the environment and their livelihoods.

5. Trashigang: Located in eastern Bhutan, Trashigang is one of the largest districts in the country. My cleaning campaigns here have involved numerous community members who are eager to participate. The warm hospitality of the people has made it a memorable part of my journey.

Each of these locations has contributed to my understanding of the diverse challenges we face in waste management and the importance of community engagement in creating lasting change.

FACING DOUBTS AND EMBRACING MY MISSION

Throughout my journey, there were moments when people questioned my sanity. Many did not understand why I was so passionate about picking up trash and engaging in environmental advocacy. Friends and family sometimes expressed concern, wondering if my dedication was a sign of instability. However, as they observed my commitment and the changes we were making in our community, their perspectives began to shift. They started to see that my mission was not just about cleaning; it was about fostering a deeper respect for our environment and instilling a sense of responsibility in those around us.

Coming from Nabji, again, a remote village that holds cultural significance as the entry point of Guru Rinpoche into Bhutan, I was raised with a strong sense of community and connection to nature. My parents, who instilled in me the importance of caring for our surroundings, often reminded me of our responsibilities as stewards of the Earth. They inspired me to respect our land and heritage, which ultimately fueled my desire to protect our environment for future generations.

IMPORTANT PEOPLE IN MY LIFE

Throughout my journey, there have been several key individuals who have inspired and supported me. Their encouragement has been crucial to my mission, and I want to take a moment to acknowledge their contributions.

1. **My wife, Ugyen Tshomo:** My greatest support, Ugyen has stood by me through every challenge. Her unwavering belief in my mission has provided me with the emotional strength and encouragement I need to keep going. She embodies the spirit of community and compassion, reminding me that our work is about more than just cleaning; it's about fostering a sense of responsibility toward our environment and each other.

2. **My children:** My three sons, Jurmi Sharab Gembo, Ugyen Pelzang Gembo, and Jigmi Tenzin Choeda, along with my daughter, Karma Euphalma, are a source of joy and inspiration. Their curiosity and enthusiasm for nature have motivated me to work harder for a cleaner, healthier environment for future generations. Seeing them actively participate in our cleanup efforts fills me with hope for a brighter future, where they will continue the legacy of environmental stewardship.

3. **Khenchen Tandin Sithup:** The teachings of Khenchen Tandin Sithup have profoundly influenced my approach to environmental advocacy. His emphasis on mindfulness and

compassion aligns closely with my own beliefs. During my visits to various monasteries, Khenchen has shared insights on how we can integrate Buddhist principles into our waste management efforts. His encouragement to view waste not merely as a physical problem but as a spiritual challenge has helped me frame my mission within a deeper context.

4. **Fellow guides:** My fellow tour guides have played a significant role in shaping my journey. Many of them have embraced the idea of environmental advocacy, joining me in cleanup campaigns and spreading awareness among their guests. Together, we have formed a supportive network that seeks to educate visitors about Bhutan's unique environment and the importance of preserving it.

5. **Community volunteers:** The local volunteers who join me on cleanup drives are the backbone of my efforts. These individuals, including students, teachers, and farmers, dedicate their time to support our campaigns. Their commitment to maintaining the cleanliness of our land is heartening. Together, we have fostered a sense of community that transcends individual efforts.

6. **Local authorities and NGOs:** Collaboration with local authorities and non-governmental organizations (NGOs) has been crucial in promoting waste management initiatives. They provide resources and support for our campaigns, helping to amplify our

message. Their involvement has helped us reach a broader audience and implement more effective strategies for waste reduction.

THE CAMPAIGN JOURNEY CONTINUES

As I continued my journey through the various districts of Bhutan, each location offered unique challenges and opportunities for growth. In each place, I witnessed the profound impact of community engagement on environmental awareness.

In Thimphu, I organized workshops in schools, where students learned about waste management and environmental stewardship. The enthusiasm of the young participants was infectious, and many of them expressed a desire to start their own initiatives within their communities. Their eagerness to take action reaffirmed my belief that the younger generation holds the key to a sustainable future.

In Bumthang, I collaborated with local monks to organize a community cleanup around the sacred Jakar Dzong. The monks' presence added a spiritual dimension to our efforts, reinforcing the idea that caring for our environment is a form of respect for our spiritual heritage. The local community turned out in full force, and together, we collected over 1,000 kilograms of waste in just a few hours.

Throughout my campaigns, I have encountered challenges—harsh weather, difficult terrains, and sometimes even apathy from those who do not understand the urgency of our mission. Yet, each obstacle has reinforced my determination to continue. The support from my family, friends, and community members has been a guiding light during these difficult times, reminding me that I am not alone in this journey.

REFLECTIONS AND LESSONS LEARNED

Reflecting on my journey, both as a guide and a waste advocacy leader, I recognize how deeply this experience has impacted me on personal and professional levels. What began as a mission to clean up our country has grown into something far more meaningful, transforming the way I see my role in society.

On a professional level, being a guide allowed me to appreciate the natural beauty of Bhutan. However, as I walked across different regions picking up trash, I realized that guiding people to experience this beauty wasn't enough. I had to take action to protect it. This journey opened my eyes to the importance of leading by example and educating people about environmental stewardship. It made me more aware of the significance of integrating waste management advocacy into my work as a guide. Now, I not only show people the wonders of Bhutan but also encourage them to respect and preserve it.

Personally, this journey has been nothing short of transformative. I've faced countless physical challenges—treacherous roads, heavy rains, leeches, landslides, and long stretches of solitude. There were moments when I questioned my own sanity, as people stared at me, puzzled by my mission to pick up garbage. My parents, who raised me with care after I lost my mother at a young age, worried that I wasn't meant for such work. Yet here I am, doing the necessary but often overlooked task of picking up trash and cleaning.

Through all of this, I found purpose and strength that I never knew existed within me. The constant support of my wife, children, and community helped me keep going, even when the road got tough. The pride I feel in knowing that I've collected over 95,000 kilograms of garbage is immense, but even greater is the joy of seeing others join me in this cause.

The emotional and spiritual growth has been significant as well. Meeting kind strangers, monks, and people from all walks of life taught me humility and kindness. It reminded me that no matter the challenges, there are always helping hands and open hearts along the way. When Khenchen Tandin Sithup shared Buddha's teachings about waste management with the monks, it reinforced my belief that this work is not just about cleaning; it's about mindfulness, compassion, and responsibility for our environment.

The hardest part has been pushing through when everything seemed to go wrong, from car breakdowns to roadblocks. But each challenge taught me patience, resilience, and faith—faith that my actions, no matter how small, can spark change.

CONCLUSION

In the end, this journey has shaped me into someone who believes in the power of community and collective action. I no longer feel like a lone advocate; I'm part of a growing movement. As I continue to guide people through Bhutan, I will also guide them toward a future where we all take ownership of our country's well-being. This journey was about cleaning, but it became a path to self-discovery, reminding me that every small effort counts in making Bhutan zero waste by 2030.

I invite everyone—whether you are a visitor to our beautiful country or a fellow Bhutanese—to join me in this mission. Together, we can ensure that Bhutan remains a beacon of environmental beauty and cultural richness for generations to come. The journey is ongoing, and the responsibility is collective. Let us all commit to this noble cause and work hand in hand to create a cleaner, greener Bhutan.

Sophie Rouméas

ABOUT THE ANTHOLOGIST

Sophie Rouméas is a practitioner of holistic therapies. Driven by the transformative power of words to spark emotions, reflection, and change, she guides meditations, hypnosis sessions, and family constellations.

Through Angel Lab Éditions, Sophie aims to highlight essential themes such as solidarity, resilience, and legacy. She curates collective works that give voice to inspiring and meaningful stories. Since 2021, Sophie has published four books, including three anthologies, such as the Amazon bestseller *J'ai Vécu la Même Chose Que Toi* (*I Walked That Path Too*), where co-authors genuinely share their resilience during the challenge of breast cancer. These projects embody her dedication to providing a platform for engaged and compassionate voices. *Daring Metamorphosis* is a testament to this commitment to collective storytelling.

Born in the French Alps, Sophie draws her inspiration from nature and the love she shares with her loved ones. Through her literary and therapeutic projects, she strives to promote the values of connection and transformation. Her motto: *"Let's voice your soul!"*

Individual sessions: www.sophieroumeas.com
Healing the Family Tree: www.healingthefamilytree.com
Facebook: www.facebook.com/sophie.roumeas1/

Published Books:
J'ai Vécu la Même Chose Que Toi, 2021
I Walked That Path Too, 2023 (English version)
J'ai Vécu la Même Chose Que Toi, 2025 – Volume 2
Souls in Love, 2022 (English version)
Contributions as a Co-Author:
Step into Your Brilliance, 2019, compiled by Rebecca Hall-Gruyter
Bright Spots, 2020, compiled by Cathy Davis